SUNY Series in Environmental Public Policy
Lester W. Milbrath, Editor

ENVIRONMENTALISTS
Vanguard for a New Society

ENVIRON

Environmental Studies Center
State University of New York at Buffalo

MENTALISTS

Vanguard
for a New Society

LESTER W. MILBRATH
WITH THE ADVICE AND ASSISTANCE OF
BARBARA V. FISHER

State University of New York Press

ALBANY

Published by
State University of New York Press, Albany
© 1984 State University of New York
All rights reserved
Printed in the United States of America
No part of this book may be used or reproduced
in any manner whatsoever without written permission
except in the case of brief quotations embodied in
critical articles and reviews.

For information, address State University of New York
Press, State University Plaza, Albany, N.Y., 12246

Library of Congress Cataloging in Publication Data

Milbrath, Lester W.
  Environmentalists: Vanguard for a New Society.

  (SUNY series in environmental public policy)
  Includes bibliographical references.
  1. Environmental policy. 2. Social change.
I. Fisher, Barbara V. II. Title. III. Series.
HC79.E5M47 1984   363.7   83–24250
ISBN 0–87395–887–X
ISBN 0–87395–888–8 (pbk.)

10 9 8 7 6 5 4

Contents

Tables

Figures

Preface

My main purpose in writing this book was to try to help the reader to see his world, and how it works, in a new way. I can't be certain that my vision of reality is the correct one but there is a good deal of evidence to support it. Some readers may question that evidence, but I hope they will be challenged to gather additional evidence so that all of us can become better informed. The book is addressed to interested laypersons, public officials, and upper division undergraduates as well as to scholars. To facilitate easy reading and clear development of an argument, the description of the study on which the book is based, as well as many of the statistical tables, has been placed in the appendices.

In an ultimate sense, this is a book about our civilization, the human condition and quality of life. There is no way for a scholar to inquire into the human condition or into the capacity of his civilization to provide quality of life for its people without identifying major deficiencies that cry out for recommendations for improvement. Some areas of study are inherently "radicalizing." This thrust is even stronger if the analyst projects from the past and the present into the future. Therefore, this is not only a scholarly book but also a book with a point of view. I intend to challenge my readers and I expect to stir up controversy. If that helps us to understand a little better who we are, where we are at, and where we would like to go, I will have achieved my purpose.

Acknowledgments

Many of the ideas and much of the evidence in this book derived from a comparative three-nation study of environmental beliefs and values. Teams of scholars in England, Germany, and the United States worked together in designing the project, executing it, and analyzing and writing up the results. Hans Kessel and Hans Joachim Fietkau on the staff of the International Institute for Environment and Society, part of the Science Center in Berlin, made especially significant contributions. Stephen Cotgrove and Andrew Duff of the Department of Sociology at the University of Bath in England also made significant conceptual and analytical contributions. The U.S.A. team worked out of the Environmental Studies Center at the State University of New York at Buffalo. From that team I am especially indebted to Martha Cornwell, Jeff Coopersmith, and L. Gardner Shaw; also Rosemary Maziarz, Deirdre Gordon, Marc Sherman, and Anne Hildreth.

More than anyone else, I am indebted to Barbara Fisher; she worked with me at every phase of the project from its inception to the final draft of the book. She provided many conceptual ideas, she helped draft and later typed questionnaires, she assisted and supervised all of the mailings, she helped process the information as it was received, she kept the books, she helped interpret the meaning of data, she advised me on the conceptual structure of the book, she critiqued and edited my writing, and she typed more drafts than she or I wish to remember. In short, she has been invaluable.

Lee Botts, Margaret Wooster, and Ben Agger were kind enough to read drafts of the manuscript and share their comments with me. Riley Dunlap, a reader for the SUNY Press, also made a number of very helpful suggestions.

ONE

We Are at a Fork in the Road

As we "Westerners" think about prophets, we are likely to call up images from the Old Testament of wise men predicting the future. Their predictions often were accompanied by dire warnings that unless people changed their ways God would be displeased and their lives would be filled with much pain and sadness. The people looked to these prophets as authoritative interpreters of how the world works and also of how people should behave. Most environmentalists do not think of themselves as prophets but, like prophets of old, they warn the people that they must change their ways if they wish to have a good life. Consider the following:

1) In April, 1983, a U.S. national news network ran a story showing a wisp of a girl with flowing red hair in a rubber raft with an outboard motor carrying a "Greenpeace" banner. She was circling around a large vessel off the coast of Los Angeles that was engaged in the early stages of exploration for offshore drilling of oil. As the media filmed the dramatic scene, she called out with a bullhorn to the people on the vessel to cease their activities and did her best to disrupt them. Greenpeace is a militant environmental organization that has used confrontational tactics to try to stop whaling, killing of seal pups, offshore oil and gas drilling and production, and so forth. They believe that the many forms of sea life are seriously threatened by the intrusive activities of humans. They are opposed by people who wish to use the resources of the seas and seabeds for human purposes even if those activities should result in injury or even destruction of other species. There is a clear conflict in values between the two groups, who are operating from very different beliefs about the proper relationship between humans and nature.

2) Tasmania is a lush island south of mainland Australia with approximately 450,000 inhabitants. The people there live a tranquil life, far removed from many of the cares of the rest of the world, but they also experience high unemployment. Some of them believe that they should more fully exploit their natural resources to build up their industry, provide jobs and get richer. In the southwest sector of the island, the Franklin River flows through a remote and lovely valley where there is a unique temperate rain forest that was declared a "World Heritage" area by UNESCO.

The Hydro-Electric Commission of the State of Tasmania covets the hydroelectric potential for the valley and decided to build a dam and power project there that would have the effect of destroying this unique

1

ecosystem. The Tasmanian Wilderness Society was originally formed in 1976 to save the Franklin River. It organized a coalition of 16 major conservation groups. This Wilderness Society announced plans for a non-violent blockade of the project in July 1982. The blockade commenced in Dec. 1982. Over the next few months more than 2600 people joined the action and 1272 were arrested; naturally it drew worldwide media attention. When a federal election was called on Feb. 3, 1983, the Coalition announced that it would campaign for the Labor Party.

The environmentalists concentrated their electioneering in key districts and won a resounding victory. Robert J. Hawke, the leader of the Labor Party, and the newly elected Prime Minister, promised the day after his election on March 5, 1983, that the dam "will not be built."

3) Amory Lovins, an experimental physicist working with the "Friends of the Earth" organization, has become a leading advocate of an alternative energy policy. He particularly attracted attention by publishing an article in foreign affairs in 1976 with the title, "Energy Strategy: The Road Not Taken?" This was followed by publication of a book titled, *Soft Energy Paths: Toward a Durable Peace* (1977). Lovins advocates scaling down the energy needs of modern society by using conserving technologies and behavior and by developing many dispersed, smaller, and more manageable sources of energy (such as solar heating, windmills, and small hydro) rather than gigantic technologically complex and potentially damaging installations (such as nuclear power plants). The dispute over "soft" vs. "hard" energy paths is not only over the best way to get the energy we "need" but also over the kind of society in which the disputants would like to live.

4) The Ogallala Aquifer is a gigantic underground aquifer (fresh water reservoir) underlying a large portion of the plains states from Texas north to the Dakotas. Humans learned a few decades ago that fresh water could be brought to the surface for irrigation by using gigantic electrically-powered pumps. These irrigated lands have become so productive and created so much wealth in a semi-arid part of the United States that others are attracted to the activity and nearly everyone who can is sinking wells to tap into this great resource. The exploitive use of this resource is becoming a "tragedy of the commons" as each well-holder extracts all the wealth he can with little regard for the common good. The aquifer is drying up and the agri-businesses that face displacement are now casting about vigorously to find alternative sources of fresh water. Their attention naturally has focused on the Great Lakes Basin since it contains the largest amount of surface fresh water available anywhere on the planet. They propose building a canal from Lake Superior across Minnesota and over to the plains states. Given the power that modern humans command, such a project is technologically feasible. Environmentalists, particularly those in the Great Lake Basin, dispute the wisdom of such an action, claiming that large

scale diversion of fresh water from the basin would seriously damage the ecosystem as well as weaken the economic base of the people who live in the basin. Researchers currently are busily calculating the costs and benefits of such a project but the more basic question is how we should relate to nature as we conduct our lives; the dispute finally will be settled by political means.

5) The natural biological life (aquatic animals and plants) of many lakes in Northeast Canada and the United States has been stunted, or killed off altogether, by a phenomenon called acid precipitation. While some of this "acid rain" is produced by automobile exhausts, it is believed that the largest contributors are electric power plants burning cheap high sulphur coal; especially those in the Ohio Valley. Their emissions contain sulphur dioxide that, when carried aloft and mixed with water vapor, turns into sulphuric acid and falls hundreds of miles away in the form of acid precipitation. In order to meet local air pollution standards, many of these plants have built exceedingly tall smoke stacks to disperse the pollutants; but this tactic thrusts the SO_2 high into the clouds and thus produces even more acid rain. Acid precipitation is causing considerable damage to the fishing and tourism industries in Canada and has led to a major dispute between Canada and the United States. Early in the Reagan administration, when environmentalists and the governments of the affected areas pressed the U.S. government to take vigorous action to stop acid rain, David Stockman, the Director of the Budget, traded off the two values by inquiring why people should have to pay higher electric rates to save a few fish. This choice illustrates the divergent ways humans see themselves relating to nature.

6) Love Canal was dug by William Love in the 1890's in an attempt to divert water from the Niagara River over the escarpment to an electric power plant that would provide energy for a new industrial city. Financial setbacks brought the project to a close after only about a mile of the canal had been dug. Later, Hooker Chemical Company purchased the land and buried chemical wastes in the canal during the 1930's and 40's. During the 50's, homes were built in the area and the Niagara Falls School Board bought the dumpsite (which had been capped with clay), where they subsequently built a school and playground.

By the 1970's, many of the steel drums that enclosed the chemicals had corroded and the contents leaked out, mixed with that of other chemicals in the dump, and leached laterally through the soil to the basements of nearby homes. Residents in the area began to notice health effects during the 1970's, and in 1978 not only the residents but the whole world learned that the chemicals in Love's canal were seriously injuring the people who lived there. The State Health Commissioner ordered the school closed and the neighborhood residents formed a "Love Canal Homeowners Association." This was the opening salvo in a long series of altercations between citizens and their governments as they struggled to mitigate the calamity that had befallen these innocent people (Levine, 1982). In May 1980, shortly after a chromosomal study was released to the residents suggesting that many of them may have suffered chromosomal damage, the Homeowners Association dramatized their grievance by holding two EPA officials hostage. Both the state and the federal governments were forced into making new policies for protecting people from toxic chemical waste by the series of dramatic episodes at Love Canal.

Disparate as these vignettes are in place and topic, they have a great deal in common. In each case, and in many other thousands that could be cited, there is a story of people rising up to tell their fellows that we have been abusing our environment and threatening the balance of our ecosystems. Just like the prophets of old, they are urging us to change our ways, to choose a new direction at the fork in the road, if we wish to continue having a good life on this planet. Having the capability to do something does not necessarily justify our proceeding to do it. Our knowledge and power enable us to dominate other species and set us apart from them; yet, our very success could become our failure, say these prophets. Dinosaurs lived on this planet for about 550 million years while humans have lived here for only 2 or 3 million years. How is it then, in such a relatively short period of time, that humans have come to dominate life on earth so completely? What are the chances that humans can live on this planet as long as dinosaurs?

Throughout most of their existence on this planet, humans have lived in hunter/gatherer societies that minimally disturbed the biosphere. They believed that humans had to be adaptive and adjusted their lifestyle to the demands of nature. The agricultural revolution that began about 10,000 years ago in the Middle East, Asia, and Europe led humans to develop a more exploitive role toward nature. They learned to raise plants and animals specifically to meet human needs. Modest alterations of ecosystems, such as irrigation or flood control, were undertaken to further adapt the environment to human needs. In these agricultural/small-city cultures, the belief that humans should adapt to nature persisted but the alternative belief that humans could manipulate and alter nature for their own purposes also was growing. Most of the world's great religions were spawned in this era.

Over the past 400 years, humans have experienced another fundamental revolution in their relationship to nature; the scientific-technical-industrial revolution has made it possible for humans to take an increasingly "exuberant" role toward nature. My use of the concept "exuberance" is taken from Catton (*Overshoot*, 1980) who defines ecological exuberance as "the lavish use of resources by members of a freely expanding population" that can lead to an optimistic, almost euphoric, mood. Humans have used their science, knowledge, imagination, and tools to extract materials from nature and to dominate nature in ways that would have been incomprehensible to our forebearers. We can travel around the planet with amazing swiftness, we can level mountains, change the course of rivers, clear away gigantic forests, and alter climates. We can develop, store, and transmit information with the speed of light; our capability for collective memory and thinking allows us to understand phenomena, tackle problems, and create solutions that were unimaginable only a generation ago. We have come to expect constant change, but change is accelerating so quickly that many people feel that their heads are reeling.

As people ponder a number of developments, and look to the future, they are coming to realize that the exuberant posture of humans toward nature is producing some unfortunate consequences. The agricultural and industrial revolutions have enabled human population to grow at an unprecedented pace. Currently the gain of births over deaths, worldwide, is about 70 million per year. If the present rate of population growth were to continue into the future as long as the elasped time since the beginning of the industrial revolution, there would be only about 1.5 square yards of exposed land surface for each person. Obviously, such a thing would never happen because humans would experience "die off" long before that density could develop. It does demonstrate, however, that humans must find some way to control population growth. Some observers believe that the human species already is in an overgrowth situation that biologists call "overshoot" (Catton, 1980).

As population has grown, so has the rate of resource consumption. We have already extracted from the earth's crust most of the readily obtainable minerals and fossil energy. These constitute a kind of "ghost acreage" that enables humans to produce more food and other consumer goods than would be possible without the use of fossil energy (Catton, 1980). We must now search for minerals and energy in more difficult and dangerous locations and transport them over long distances, at a significantly increased risk to ourselves and our biosphere. Environmental prophets warn that since minerals and energy are in finite supply, our descendants face the prospect of severe shortages of food, minerals, and energy. As more and more people compete for few resources, prices are likely to rise and the overall material standard of living is likely to decline.

Not only are we growing faster and using things up more swiftly, say the prophets, but we are crowding other species out of their niches (Ehrlich and Ehrlich, 1981). We are slashing down forests, flooding river valleys, putting every possible bit of land into cultivation, and inadvertently creating deserts. Furthermore, we are poisoning our environment with our wastes; in many areas the air is unhealthy to breathe, the water is unhealthy to drink, and our food may be contaminated. We are discovering that many of our products and by-products are harmful to us instead of nurturing our good health, happiness, and well being. We can unleash sufficient nuclear energy to obliterate most life on this planet. At the same time that humans rejoice and feel proud of their ability to dominate nature, there are nagging doubts that we may not be on the right road to a high quality of life. Does the swift development of our species carry the seeds of our own destruction?

Prophecy and Society Choice

In most primitive communities, the prophets (chiefs, priests, wise men, witch doctors) who interpreted for their people how the world works, usually claimed that a god or other spirits determine the workings of nature and the fortunes of humans as they live in nature. These "wise men" had the ability to remember and preserve that which was believed to be good from the past, and to prescribe "correct" forms of behavior in the present that the people were told would provide a happy and fulfilling future. These prophets urged their people to adopt certain beliefs and behavior that assuredly would lead to eternal life in some future heaven. Their interpretations as to how the world works were given authority by mystical connections to an infallible, all-powerful god that not only told humans what they must do but also could shape nature itself, for it was this very god that had created nature. Even though we moderns are skeptical of the pretentious claims to know how the world works put forth by the prophets of old, we can recognize the importance for social cohesion of having an agreed upon "story" that guides the beliefs and behavior of the people.

In modern society there are no widely recognized infallible prophets to tell us how the world works and how we should behave. Science is now being looked to as the authority to tell us how our natural world works, although we are continually discovering how much we still do not know. In addition, science and technology have given humans the power and capability to do many things that have far-reaching social, economic and political consequences, some of which may be life-threatening. Yet, the canons of science lead scientists to strive to keep it value free; furthermore, scientists will not try to give society a code of ethics. Instead, we fall back on an ethical code, inherited from organized religion, that was mainly developed in a pre-scientific era when humans had less capability to dominate and exploit nature. Our ethical/normative structure is so far out of step with the power and capability provided by modern science than many people are questioning the wisdom of following the normative prescriptions from old traditions. Many of them believe that these old traditions are incapable of guiding us as we strive presently to avoid destroying our own biosphere and civilization.

It would be helpful if today's society could find some modern-day prophets who understand, much better than ever before, how the world works physically and socially and who also have the breadth and depth of vision to develop a new ethical/normative belief structure that would enable humans to so guide their affairs, and redirect the course of their society, that they could live lives of reasonably high quality in a long-run sustainable relationship with nature. A new group of leaders, known simply as environmentalists, is trying to combine a sophisticated understanding of the natural workings of the world with a newly developing environmentally-oriented ethic. These leaders have the potential for becoming modern-day prophets to guide society toward a better way of life, one that is sustainable in nature over the long run. This book is an examination of their role in modern society as they attempt to fulfill the mission they have chosen.

Mindless Pursuit of "Progress" in the Old Dominant Social Paradigm

A paradigm may be defined as a society's dominant belief structure that organizes the way that people perceive and interpret the functioning of the world around them. Thomas Kuhn (1962), a philosopher/ historian of science, has elucidated the way that scientific disciplines or communities are dominated by an accepted belief paradigm that shapes the way the people participating in that discipline think about their subject matter. From time to time, paradigms are proven to be faulty in certain respects and they undergo a shift toward a new, more adequate paradigm. Such shifts generally are resisted strongly and occur only when the old paradigm has proved to be no longer serviceable or acceptable. Schwartz and Ogilvy (1979) suggest that paradigm shift is occuring in many academic disciplines at the present time.

The idea of a dominant paradigm can be applied to cultures or societies, as well as to scientific disciplines; in such cases we refer to them as dominant social paradigms. Every organized society has a dominant social paradigm (DSP) which consists of the values, metaphysical beliefs, institutions, habits, etc., that collectively provide social lenses through which individuals and groups interpret their social world. Social paradigms condition individual goals and expectations, provide a definition of social problems, establish a structure of social and physical rewards for various types of preferred behavior, and create shared gains and deprivations which make social harmony in complex societies possible (Pirages, 1982, p. 6).

A social paradigm contains the survival information needed for the maintenance of a culture. It results from generations of social learning whereby dysfunctional values and beliefs are discarded in favor of those more suited to collective survival. It is extremely difficult to dislodge important elements of a dominant social paradigm once it becomes firmly entrenched because individual integrity and socially shared definitions of reality are anchored in it (Pirages, 1982, p.7). Nearly all of the values, norms, beliefs and institutions of the society are oriented toward maintenance of the paradigm.

> [A paradigm] is dominant not in the statistical sense of being held by most people, but in the sense that it is the paradigm held by dominant groups in industrial societies; and in the sense that it

serves to legitimate and justify the institutions and practices of a market economy. . . . it is the taken-for-granted common-sensical view which usually determines the outcome of debates on environmental issues. (Cotgrove, 1982, p. 27)

Paradigms are not only beliefs about what the world is like and guides to action; they also serve the function of legitimating or justifying courses of action. That is to say, they function as ideologies. . . . Hence, conflicts over what constitutes the paradigm by which action should be guided and judged to be reasonable is *[sic]* itself a part of the political process. The struggle to universalize a paradigm is part of the struggle for power. (Cotgrove, 1982, p. 88)

As solid as such structures of beliefs, values and institutions may seem, they *do change* over time for reasons that we only partially understand. The social structures built around slavery and colonialism have crumbled and given way to new structures that reject those once accepted patterns for relationships among people. The beliefs about the proper relationship between humans and nature are, if anything, more fundamental than the beliefs about the proper relationships among people. We noted above that the transformation of human societies from a predominantly hunter/gatherer mode to an agricultural mode was accompanied by a change from the belief that humans must adapt to nature to the belief that humans could alter nature to meet their needs. The scientific-technical-industrial revolution, in turn, was accompanied by a belief that humans could dominate nature and control it to suit their purposes.

Characteristics of the 20th-Century Industrial Dominant Social Paradigm

Catton and Dunlap (1980) postulate that the "dominant western worldview" rests on the following four basic beliefs:

1) People are fundamentally different from all other creatures on earth over which they have dominion.
2) People are masters of their destiny; they can choose their goals and learn to do whatever is necessary to achieve them.
3) The world is vast, and thus provides unlimited opportunities for humans.
4) The history of humanity is one of progress; for every problem there is a solution, and thus progress need never cease.

Notice the emphasis that is placed on man's superiority in nature.

This exuberant posture of humans toward nature becomes translated at a more concrete level into the following premises about the way that we should structure our society and conduct our public business:

1) Good economic conditions (generally this means economic growth) ought to be the dominant object of public policy.
2) Science and technology are to be revered and promoted because they can be used to dominate nature and accumulate material wealth.
3) Promoting new technology and enterprises to extract even more from nature and accumulate more wealth entails physical and social risks which society should encourage.
4) Society works best if people are differentially rewarded for skills, initiative, and achievement as this will maximize productivity; rewarding people equally depresses productivity and wealth.
5) Decisional structures and practices of a society must be oriented toward efficiency and decisiveness; it is inefficient to let many people have a say in decisions because it slows things down too much and prevents us from "getting on with the job."
6) The supply and demand market is the best mechanism for regulating economic relationships; hence, it is best to minimize regulation and taxes. The public good is better served when people use their own resources in the competition of the market place. Since the market works very adequately for assuring the public good, it is bad policy for public agencies to use forecasting and planning to try to bring about the public good.
7) The socio-economic system works best if it is oriented to maximize the wealth of individuals now living; there is no need to be concerned about future generations since the market will work things out when that time comes. (This is claimed despite the fact that the market has no mechanism to register the demands of future members of the species.)

These beliefs are stated in extreme form to accent their coherent structure and central emphasis; they represent a polar position usually identified with the "right" in modern industrial societies. Some of these beliefs, particularly numbers 4, 6, and 7 with their emphasis on the market, have been challenged from the "left" (Marxists, Socialists, and Communists). It is important to note, however, that the other four beliefs as well as those identified by Catton and Dunlap, are accepted by the "left." Both left and right adopt the same fundamental posture that humans should dominate nature. Some contemporary "Neo-Marxists" are re-interpreting Marx to incorporate a more protective stance toward nature (Agger, 1979). Examination of the practices of modern society also discloses that we do not carry out DSP beliefs in their pure form: wealth is not the only object of public policy; we do try to protect people from risk; we open many decisions to input from the public even if it slows things down; the market system is modified by an overlay of regulation, taxes, and provision for the future. It is ironic, however, that the political coalitions that recently (early '80's) won power in England, the United States, and Germany espoused a return to the fundamental premises of the DSP identified above.

Despite the current political dominance of the DSP perspective, increasing numbers of people in advanced industrial societies have come to doubt the validity of these premises. Their doubts and their challenge go even deeper than the challenge from the left because they are questioning and challenging the basic structure and purpose of modern industrial society.

The Challenge to the Old DSP

Several overlapping social thrusts (e.g. the environmental movement, the peace movement, the women's movement, and the civil rights movement) in modern industrial societies are challenging the validity of the old DSP. The following are some of the considerations cited by those who vigorously object to the way that modern society is working:

1) A society working according to the old DSP generates great differences in wealth and opportunity; these differences are so extensive that many people believe them to be unjust.

2) Unbridled industrial activity has generated dangerous pollution and has inflicted serious damage to nature that may be irreversible.

3) Many people have been put at risk and seriously injured because of the negligent acts of persons and firms who are only acting normally within the old DSP to maximize their own wealth.

4) Natural resources are being depleted so swiftly that we now face serious shortages, high inflation, and the prospect that our children will have no choice but to accept a lower material standard since there will be insufficient resources to go around at present consumption levels.

5) Many of the "entitlements" (social security, unemployment benefits, etc.) that people have come to expect because of high rates of economic growth over the past several decades, very likely can no longer be sustained by our economic system. Being cheated out of one's "entitlement" is far more difficult to handle psychologically than suffering the whims of capricious nature (floods, tornadoes, crop failure, etc.).

6) Humans now possess the capability, through nuclear weapons, to destroy the whole human race as well as most of the other species in the biosphere. It requires only one breakdown in social control for this awesome power to be unleashed.

7) Quality of life studies have shown that a person's ability to achieve control of his own fate is an important element for

realizing quality of life. Modern society is so complicated and crowded that it is difficult for most people to achieve a satisfactory level of personal fate control within the market system. Economic forces inflict on the average individual such evils as inflation, unemployment, pollution, and widespread uncertainty about the future. Control over these forces can only be realized in concert with others as a collective good. Many people have a sense of losing, or of already having lost, control of their lives. They perceive that they are buffeted and controlled by forces that they cannot understand and that they have no hope of influencing. In modern society, particularly in America, people may achieve private affluence but they are subjected to public squalor. They would like to turn to the government to improve the collective components of their lives but at the very time when government is most needed, it is increasingly disabled because our national consensus is dissolving (see Chapter 2).

If the society, working according to the old DSP, is experiencing such difficult problems, why don't we simply change it? While most people feel that modern society does indeed have many of the difficulties just mentioned, there also are many things that people feel are good about modern society. Inhabitants of advanced industrial countries have been relieved of a great deal of the heavy physical drudgery that their forebearers had to endure. Modern medicine makes it possible for people to recover from or cope with many of the injuries and illnesses that shortened the lives of their ancestors. Even ordinary people now have the opportunity to travel to exotic places, to experience the thrill of power (e.g. drive through wilderness in an off-road vehicle), to eat exotic food that formerly only the nobles could afford, to bring the best entertainment in the world into their own living rooms. The list could be extended, but you get the idea. At one level of analysis it is valid to say that humans never had it so good. Ironically, it is the very achievements of modern science and technology, such as those just mentioned, that eventuates in the sense of unease about the way society is working that was spelled out in the seven points delineated above. For example, travel by masses of people to exotic places not only destroys their exotic character but consumes prodigious amounts of fossil energy. When the energy is depleted, such travel will no longer be possible and many other energy dependent activities also will be impossible. The very success of modern society could well lead to its failure.

Why don't we keep what is good about modern society and fix up those things that aren't working well? At first blush that sounds eminently sensible. Some people believe that the major problems of modern society can be solved by developing more and better technology. Many others, however, are persuaded that the fundamental problems of society are not reachable by technology; they believe that fundamental social change is required. As we shall see later in the book, this basic difference in the diagnosis of our society's ills is a major distinguishing characteristic between contending groups in our policy. No doubt technological development will continue but, if our social problems are as deeply embedded in our culture as the environmentalists claim they are, technological development will not be sufficient for their solution.

Even if technology alone can't solve our social problems, why don't we try to get people to change the way they behave? Normative-ethical systems based in religion have traditionally been used throughout human history to guide the behavior of people. Most of the religiously based ethical systems that command a wide following today were developed many centuries ago when humans had much less power and capability to dominate nature. Most of these religions set humans apart from other animals granting humans the "right" to dominate and control nature. Because the prophets of old could not anticipate the power and exuberance that modern technology would place in the hands of humans, our religious heritage provides little guidance for problems like the following:

1) Human population is growing so swiftly that its numbers must be limited either by interference with normal reproduction (birth control or abortion) or by premature death (disease or famine).
2) Humans can distort or obliterate the biosphere (slash down forests, move mountains, redirect rivers, etc.), foreclosing its use for other purposes.
3) Humans crowd many other species out of their niches and drive some of them to extinction.
4) Humans can, through nuclear war, devastate much of the planet's biosphere and destroy all life in those areas.
5) A minority of the world's population, located in a few privileged countries, can dig out, and use up, in a few centuries most of the planet's storehouse of metals and fossil energy.
6) Humans can invent new life forms.
7) Humans can keep bodies "alive" even though the brain is "dead."

No, turning back to old moral precepts will not solve the problems of modern society.

Changing the way we behave is difficult for another reason. Our technological/industrial structure carries a momentum and an imperative that is almost irresistible; we can't slow down or stop even if we would like to. Our ethical understanding is insufficiently developed to control the behavior of modern corporations, technological development, or nations.

Automobile manufacturing in the United States provides an example of this paradox. Although automobiles provide such important advantages for people as freedom in getting about, they also profligately use up our precious resources, they pollute the air, they get clogged in traffic jams, they contribute an exceedingly high accidental injury and death rate, and they seem to dominate our lives. Even though we already have plenty of them, we feel compelled to keep turning out new cars at a prodigious rate in order to avoid cutbacks and unemployment in the auto industry that would also create generally poor economic conditions and considerable unemployment in supportive industries (such as steelmaking).

Our leaders feel compelled to press for continued economic growth, even though it may be unattainable, because we do not have adequate social mechanisms for finding ways to meaningfully use the talents of people who lose their jobs when there is a slowdown in economic activity. The pressures of the competitive market require business firms to cut costs and discard unneeded workers; thus dumping on the larger society the responsibility to care for them. Paradoxically, our economic system is less inclined to serve the needs of all the people who live and work within it and is more inclined to serve the unquestioned goal of increasing material output. How did it happen that we developed a technical-industrial-economic system that dominates the people instead of the people being able to dominate and control it?

Technical development combined with fierce competition presents the most unstoppable of juggernauts. Scientific and economic institutions feel that they must develop new technology in order to keep ahead of the competition. If a new technology is under development, we feel we must proceed to production, even though it may present some risks and even though we are not sure that it will provide benefits that outweigh the problems and costs associated with its development and use. If we don't move ahead, another country (e.g. Japan or Russia) will develop the technology and we will fall behind in our struggle to maintain world leadership. This same reasoning is used by competitive companies.

Many humans now wish fervently that we had never developed nuclear weapons and nuclear power, but we felt we had to before the Germans or the Russians did. National pride and national competition forced the English, the French, and the Russians to develop supersonic airliners even though they are wasteful and engender more costs than benefits; it is now generally conceded that that technology was a failure. It has been estimated that American chemical companies develop approximately 3,000 new chemicals per year. It is nearly impossible to screen and thoroughly evaluate so many chemicals in a year. We occasionally discover after a chemical has been produced and put in use that it poses a severe risk to the health of humans and other species.

In modern society, progress has become almost a religious precept; we often say, "We cannot stand in the way of progress." Those that attempt to do so surely will be condemned by many others. But the environmental prophets ask, is progress such a blessing that we must pursue it mindlessly? Are we achieving real progress if it results in the "fouling of our nests" ? Are we achieving real progress if our lives are driven by technological "advances" that sweep us along without our assent? Are we achieving real progress when we persist in population and resource consumption growth rates that cannot be sustained and could well result in reducing the overall carrying capacity of the planet?

Many environmentalists are urging the people in modern society to recognize that we have reached a fork in the road.[2] If we continue our present path, they say, it will lead to severe damage of the ecosystem as well as undermine the institutions and the quality of life of the people in modern society. They urge us to take a new direction that will lead to a better way of life in a long-run sustainable relationship with nature. They urge us to cast aside old notions of progress and seek "real progress" by changing our lifestyles and the fundamental way that we do things in our society. The environmentalists are studying, educating, warning people, and seeking political power to try to get modern society to alter its course.

These modern-day prophets, these environmentalists, are beginning to develop a new environmental paradigm (NEP) (Dunlap and Van Liere, 1978; Pirages and Ehrlich, 1974) that has been receiving wide and thorough discussion within the environmental movement. The supporters of the NEP have become something of a vanguard pointing the way to a better society and also pointing out the dire consequences of continuing on our old path. This does not mean they renounce all technology, all industrial production, all growth, or all material goods. They are, however, advocating thoughtful consideration of where we are going, careful and subdued production and consumption, conservation of resources, protection of the environment, and the basic values of compassion, justice, and quality of life.

This NEP is so challenging to the old DSP that it has stimulated a rearguard effort to defend the old DSP. These competing paradigms are highly contrastive; "the protagonists face each other in a spirit of exasperation, talking past each other with mutual incomprehension. It is a dialogue of the blind talking to the deaf. Nor can the debate be settled by appeals to the facts. We need to grasp the implicit cultural meanings which underlie the dialogue." (Cotgrove, 1982, p. 33)

> It is because protagonists to the debate approach issues from different cultural contexts, which generate different and conflicting implicit meanings, that there is mutual exasperation and charges and countercharges of irrationality and unreason. What is sensible from one point of view is nonsense from another. It is the implicit, self-evident, taken-for-granted character of paradigms which clogs the channels of communication. (Cotgrove, 1982, p. 82)

In this book, we will examine the composition of this vanguard of modern day prophets, their organization and tactics, and the role they play in the politics of modern society as they try to stimulate that society to change its direction. Information for this inquiry will be drawn partly from the writings of other scholars and observers, partly from personal experience, but, rather substantially, from findings of a three-nation (England, Germany, and the United States) study of environmental beliefs and values that was first conducted in 1980 and repeated in 1982.

The Three-nation Study of Environmental Beliefs and Values

Researchers from the International Institute for Environment and Society, part of the Science Center in Berlin, the Department of Sociology at the University of Bath in England, and the Environmental Studies Center at the State Unviersity of New York at Buffalo designed and carried out a three-nation comparative study of environmental beliefs and values that had the following characteristics:

1) The research instrument (a mail questionnaire which took about 20 minutes to fill out) was made as comparable as possible in all three countries.
2) The study was longitudinal so that the development of environmental beliefs and values could be observed over time. The first two phases of the study were conducted in 1980 and 1982.
3) Information about environmental beliefs and values was sought from the broad public in each of the three countries as well as from important societal elites who were likely to be crucial actors in making environmental policy and in fostering or opposing social change with respect to environmental matters. The elite groups included environmentalists, business leaders, and public officials in each of the countries. In addition, a sample of labor leaders was drawn in the U.S. in 1980 and 1982 and in England in 1980. The U.S. study in 1980 also included a sample of media gatekeepers. (See Table 1.1 for a delineation of the groups sampled, the total number of respondents returning the questionnaire in each group, and the response rate for each group for both 1980 and 1982.)
4) The questionnaire was designed to disclose the basic belief and value structures (paradigms) that lie beneath superficial attitudes, and to show the distributions of these structures throughout the population in each of the three countries. Basic postures toward the environment as well as beliefs about specific aspects of the environmental problem, technology, political processes and social change were measured. See

TABLE 1.1
Sample Sizes and Return Rates
by Group/Each Country/Each Year

Group Sampled/by Country	1980		1982	
	Number of Respondents	Return Rate	Number of Respondents	Return Rate
United States				
General Public	1513	53.0%	695	53%
Environmentalists	225	68.0%	274	57%
Labor Leaders	85	47.0%	130	46%
Appointed Officials	153	61.0%	115	54%
Elected Officials	78	30.0%	48	22%
Business Leaders	223	49.0%	202	59%
Media Gatekeepers	105	41.0%	–	–
England				
General Public	725	42.0%	439	50%
Conservation Society	176	75.5%	365	75%
Nature Conservationists	200	82.0%	–	–
Labor Leaders	308	65.0%	–	–
Public Officials	188	38.0%	172	38%
Business Leaders	261	53.5%	247	51%
Germany				
General Public	1088	49.0%	1129	60%
Environmentalists	98	22.0%	273	47%
Public Officials	102	25.5%	111	21%
Business Leaders	130	32.5%	155	31%

Appendices A & B for copies of the questionnaires used in both years. (Personal interviews would have allowed more thorough exploration of environmental beliefs and values but insufficient funding foreclosed their use.)

The sampling procedures were quite complex and are reviewed in detail in Appendix E. Utilizing elite samples as well as the public sample sharpened belief diversity, enabling us to study the belief structures more effectively. This strategy was very useful for our study of the relationships among variables. As a sample of variance, our samples were quite effective. They were somewhat less effective in estimating the incidence of certain beliefs and their distribution through the population. Our analysis disclosed, for example, that the U.S. sample underrepresents blacks and persons from the lowest levels of education (persons who probably had difficulty understanding and completing the questionnaire). We have an excellent cross-section, however, of those people who are most likely to understand environmental questions, to play an active role in contests over environmental issues, and to be active in abetting or resisting social change. We found remarkable stability of response distributions, group by group, as we compared 1980 responses with those in 1982. This suggests that our measuring instruments and our samples were reasonably satisfactory for the task.

Having studied the data from many angles, I am quite confident that the findings to be reported in this book are a reasonably accurate estimate of the values and beliefs of people in the real world. I also believe that the story revealed here is a reasonably accurate reflection of the socio-political processes currently underway in contemporary industrialized societies. A more complete discussion of the specifics of design and sampling for the study can be found in Appendix E.

This book is not intended to be a full report of everything that we learned in the study. Most relevant to the discussion here is a set of items that measured preferred emphases for the future direction of our society. Our analysis of these and related items, which showed the presence in modern society of fairly distinct belief paradigms about how our physical and social systems work, has contributed much to our understanding of the role of environmentalists in politics and social change.

Beliefs, Behavior, and Learning

Many of the inferences about beliefs that we make in this book will be based on responses to questionnaire items. As we have reported these findings to various audiences, we have often been challenged: "How do you know that the way that people respond to a question in a questionnaire reflects what they really believe? I'll bet when it really comes to the crunch, people won't follow up by taking appropriate action." Such comments assume that there is a close linkage between belief and behavior and that the only "real" measure of belief is the way that people behave. This assumption is faulty. Beliefs can, and do, exist separately from behavior. More importantly, persons hold many beliefs simultaneously and, for any given behavior option, several beliefs may be brought to bear in making the decision. For example, the pleadings of a lover or a close friend to go off and do something that is fun could deflect even the most dedicated environmentalist from attending a meeting of his environmental group. However, the behavior (skipping the meeting) does not reflect a change in beliefs about environmentalism. Also, deciding whether or not to do something usually entails a rough calculation as to whether the expected outcome is worth the time and energy cost of doing it. If one believes that the "system" is unlikely to respond to one's efforts (as many people do these days), the potential action will not be taken even though one believes fervently that new beliefs, values and behavior patterns are needed.

Be cautious, then, about inferring from beliefs to behavior and from behavior to beliefs. Asking people what they believe is a far better basis for inferring what they "really" believe than are the inferences one could make from studying their behavior. *It is important to study both beliefs and behavior, keeping in mind their conceptual distinction, and studying the connection between them.*

It is especially important to keep these points in mind when studying people who are unlearning and relearning their beliefs, values, and behavior patterns. The changeover does not proceed at the same pace in each of these realms. We should expect, for example, that a belief and value change may occur several years in advance of a change in behavioral patterns. We all know from our own life experiences that people usually accept a new understanding at the mental level long before it is fully realized at the behavioral level. Changing from a "discarding" to a "recycling" mode of behavior takes considerable time to relearn. Abandoning the attractions of a highpowered automobile for the subdued performance of a fuel-efficient vehicle in order to conserve resources may be very difficult for a person to accept in actual behavior even though that person may recognize at an intellectual level that it will be necessary in future society. It takes many months, or years, of reinforcements and social structural support to get the mass of people in society to change basic behavior patterns. We should expect, then, that belief change is likely to be the leading edge, and considerably in advance, of behavior change.

Despite the point just made, we also should recognize that it sometimes happens that forced behavior change will lead to belief change. This is the theory behind legally enforced desegregation. It was assumed by lawmakers and judges that if it was made illegal to keep blacks and whites separated while conducting their daily business, they would eventually learn to get along together.[3] Similarly, one could argue that if polluters are no longer allowed to pollute, they will eventually learn that pollution is not a wise behavioral policy for society. The reader should recognize, then, that belief and value changes do eventually result in behavioral changes and that behavioral changes also can feed back upon beliefs and values and change them. Again, we admonish readers that it is important to measure both beliefs and behavior, keep them conceptually distinct, and look for connections between them.

The slow relearning of both beliefs and behaviors that occurs when a fundamental social change is underway leads to an interesting question: Would we know a fundamental social change while it is happening to us or would we see it only in retrospect? Did the people who experienced the agricultural revolution or the industrial revolution recognize that they were experiencing a fundamental social change? Our day-to-day lives continue in familiar patterns even though a long-term change may be occurring that, when accumulated over several decades, will amount to a fundamental revolution. Therefore, we should not expect the average person to feel that he is part of a social revolution. We must understand that in order to see a social revolution in process, we must look beneath the surface of behavior patterns, opinions, and socio-political discourse.

While thinking about this, it would be well to ask where to expect abandonment of the old DSP to occur most readily? An environmental vanguard has already abandoned the DSP and is urging the people to take a new direction (see Chapters 2 and 3). The "establishment" is likely to defend the present system; for them, the old DSP continues to work reasonably well. Most of the leadership groups in a society have a deep emotional investment, as well as strong self-interest, in the preservation of the system. They will fight to preserve the system and will be the last to abandon it. It seems, then, that the place to look for this gradual change in beliefs, and ultimately in behavior patterns, is in the large mass of people who fall somewhere between the vanguard and rearguard advocates. These people are much more ready psychologically to abandon the DSP—not necessarily because they have a vision of a better society—but because they are becoming disenchanted with the old "system" that no longer works well for them. Even though these people may not recognize the social change they are living through, many of them have already abandoned a substantial portion of the old DSP, as will be shown by the findings discussed in this book. Whether the environmentalists can attract these people to their new environmental paradigm remains to be seen. Maybe this book can help the reader to see a complex and fundamental change at work that can only be discerned as we look beneath the surface of our daily lives.

NOTES

1. The Continental Group Report (1982) shows that persons who strongly adhere to fundamentalist religion(s) in the U.S. are significantly more likely to believe that humans should exploit nature for material goods rather than preserve nature as valuable for itself.

2. Not all environmentalists urge social change, see Chapter 2. Also we recognize that there are several other groups, e.g. neo-Marxists, that criticize the old DSP and offer alternative paradigms.

3. While this policy has not been totally successful, many believe that it has had some of its intended impact.

TWO

Contrasting Belief Paradigms in Modern Society

In the previous chapter we examined the central concepts of the dominant social paradigm in modern society and we also examined some of the reasons why many people believe that paradigm is no longer serviceable. Developing a new paradigm is a difficult and slow process of consensus building. An emerging new environmental paradigm (NEP) can be discerned and various parts of it have been identified by a number of scholars (Cotgrove, 1982; Dunlap and Van Liere, 1978; Yankelovich and Lefkowitz, 1980). This emerging paradigm is receiving wide and thorough discussion within the environmental movement. After reviewing a large number of these studies, and after careful study of the findings from the three nation study, I have set forth in Table 2.1, as parsimoniously as I can, the contrasting views of the two paradigms.

The outstanding characteristics of the world view of environmentalists are their high valuation of nature, their sense of empathy which generalizes to compassion toward other species, other peoples and other generations, their desire to carefully plan and act so as to avoid risks to humans and nature, their recognition that there are limits to growth to which humans must adapt, and their desire for a new society that incorporates new ways to conduct our economic and political affairs. On each of these points, they are opposed by the defenders of the present system. Most of this chapter will be devoted to a discussion of the major components of this new paradigm and a comparison of these beliefs with those of the old DSP. In that discussion, the competing paradigms will be treated as pure types to emphasize the strong contrast between these worldviews and also to illustrate their cohesive structure.

Plotting Belief Clusters

The real world, of course, is not so neatly structured and divided. Most studies have shown that many people hold beliefs that partake of both paradigms; the reader should keep this qualifier in mind throughout the following discussion. In order to portray a variety of belief clusters, I have arrayed them in a two-dimensional space in Figure 2.1. The horizontal dimension of that space differentiates persons who resist social change from persons who strongly advocate social change. Those who resist social change generally believe that technical adjustments will suffice to deal with our environmental problems. The vertical dimension of the space contrasts people who highly value a safe, clean, and beautiful environment with those who highly value material wealth and deemphasize environmental protection.

21

TABLE 2.1

Contrast Between Competing Paradigms

New Environmental Paradigm	*Dominant Social Paradigm*

I High valuation of nature
    A) Nature for its own sake
       (worshipful love of nature)
    B) Humans harmonious with nature
    C) Environmental protection over economic growth
	1 Lower valuation of nature
	    A) Nature to produce goods
	
	    B) Human domination of nature
	    C) Economic growth over environmental protection

II Generalized compassion toward:
    A) Other species
    B) Other peoples
    C) Other generations
	II Compassion for only those near and dear
	    A) Exploitation of other species for human needs
	    B) Unconcern for other people
	    C) Concern for this generation only

III Careful planning and acting to avoid risk
    A) Science and technology not always good
    B) No further development of nuclear power
    C) Development and use of soft technology
    D) Regulation to protect nature and humans-gov't responsibility
	III Acceptance of risk to maximize wealth
	    A) Science and technology great boon to humans
	    B) Swift development of nuclear power
	    C) Emphasis on hard technology
	    D) Deemphasis on regulation-individual responsibility

IV Limits to growth
    A) Resource shortages
    B) Population explosion-limits needed
    C) Conservation
	IV No limits to growth
	    A) No resource shortages
	    B) No problem with population
	    C) Production and consumption

V Completely new society (new paradigm)
    A) Humans seriously damaging nature and themselves
    B) Openness and participation
    C) Emphasis on public goods
    D) Cooperation
    E) Post-materialism
    F) Simple lifestyles
    G) Emphasis on worker satisfaction in jobs
	V Present society okay (keep DSP)
	    A) Humans not seriously damaging nature
	
	    B) Hierarchy and efficiency
	    C) Emphasis on market
	    D) Competition
	    E) Materialism
	    F) Complex and fast lifestyles
	    G) Emphasis on jobs for economic need

VI New politics
    A) Consultative and participatory
    B) Partisan dispute over human relationship to nature
    C) Willingness to use direct action
    D) Emphasis on foresight and planning
	VI Old politics
	    A) Determination by experts
	    B) Partisan dispute over management of the economy
	    C) Opposition to direct action
	    D) Emphasis on market control

The people who resist social change and place a high valuation on material wealth have been placed in the lower right corner of the figure and have been labeled "rearguard" because they are defenders of the old DSP. At the opposite upper left corner are the "environmental reformers" in the "vanguard" who place a high valuation on a safe and clean environment and are strong advocates of social change. Many of these people have organized into vigorous groups that strive for public education about environmental problems and also utilize electoral activity and pressure group tactics to try to bring about a new environmental paradigm. Most of them eschew violence as a valid way to pursue their ends but many of them are willing to use direct actions such as protests, demonstrations, boycotts, and sit-ins to communicate their views. It is fair to say that they are one of the major social forces working for fundamental change active in American society today.

The labels "rearguard" and "vanguard" are, of course, my own. I do not intend these labels to be pejorative. The outstanding characteristic of the rearguard is that they are defenders of the DSP and the outstanding characteristic of the vanguard is that they are trying to bring about a new society. The people in the rearguard and the vanguard may not perceive themselves as such; that is beside the point. The social change that we are examining is so fundamental, and moves so slowly, that many of the actors participating in the change process, or resisting it, may not recognize the cumulative significance for the society as a whole of the changes that are occurring in their own beliefs and values as well as in the beliefs and values of others. Both sets of actors are trying to make a better world. It is up to us to understand the ways in which these worlds would be similar and the ways in which they would be different.

As indicated above, the mass of people in the United States, and in most other advanced industrial countries, partake of the beliefs of both paradigms and thus can be plotted near the center of the space in Figure 2.1. They are sympathetic toward environmental values but also hold aspirations for material wealth. On the other dimension, they have gone some distance in recognizing a need for basic social change but have not yet learned what a new, more satisfactory, social paradigm will be. They are labeled on the figure as "environmental sympathizers" because most people, in fact, do sympathize with the environmental movement. Table 1 in Appendix C reports the percentage of the United States public that agrees with or accepts the environmental perspective on twelve items that were included in the three-nation study. It can be seen in that table that three quarters or more supported the environmental perspective on most of those items. Repeated studies over the past thirteen years since Earth Day 1970 show that the level of support for environmentalism continues to be quite high despite the public's overwhelming preoccupation with economic woes in the world-wide recession of the early 1980's. A New York Times/CBS news poll

Figure 2.1   SPATIAL REPRESENTATION OF POSTURES TOWARD THE ENVIRONMENT

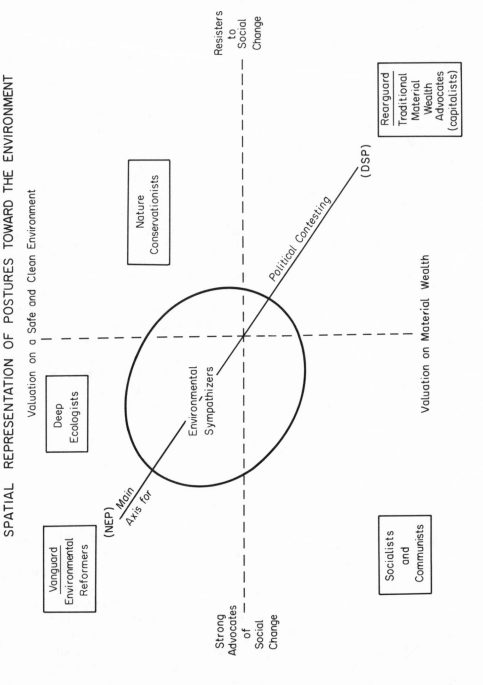

in April, 1983, showed a *rise* in support for environmental protection over the levels reported in September, 1981.

The group in the lower left quadrant labeled "socialists and communists" have long been advocates of major social change in "Western" societies but they are similar to the business/industrial sector of society in their strong emphasis on economic values and material wealth. Their main difference from the capitalists is their preference for planning and public ownership of the means of production rather than private ownership that relies on the market system to allocate goods and services. Despite struggling for many years to win adherents to their point of view, the socialists and communists have not had much success in the United States. They do not, presently, constitute a strong force for social change there.

The "left-right" dimension that has been in vogue for so many decades in characterizing political differences has less relevance for beliefs with respect to the relationship between humans and nature. Both left and right endorse a strong valuation on material wealth; therefore, the left-right dimension should be placed along the bottom of the diagram.[1] Many people, especially young people in modern industrial societies, find that left vs. right is not very relevant for characterizing their political beliefs. Interpreters and consumers of public opinion should be cautious about using the left-right dimension to characterize politics and poltical stances in modern industrial societies.[2] Even though the environmental vanguard is placed in the upper left quadrant of the figure, it should not be taken to mean they are favorable to socialism or antagonistic to capitalism. Most people in the vanguard find considerable fault with both systems, particularly their dominating emphasis on economic values.

There are quite a number of people who think of themselves as environmentalists although they do not share the strong desire for social change evident in the vanguard. We have identified those people on the diagram as "nature conservationists." They place a high valuation on a safe and clean environment but tend also to adhere to many of the beliefs, values, and social structures of modern industrial society. Many of them are politically conservative, believing that our economic and political structures are working well and should be continued. Many of them have high confidence in the ability of science and technology to solve most environmental problems. They are willing, however, to accept strong laws and regulations for protection of the environment. Many of the people in American business (even many labor leaders) fall in this category; they often call for a "balance" of environmental values and material wealth values (Continental Group Report, 1982).

The "deep ecologists" are immersed in nature emotionally and philosophically. While many "reform environmentalists" have these same deep feelings those singled out here as deep ecologists typically are not very involved in politics and political reform. Many of them live in counter-culture communities that are close to nature and minimally disturb the biosphere as they interact with nature to provide their life needs; in this sense they are both radical and conservative. Although society may eventually learn important lessons from the experiences of these people in their new communities, they do not constitute a strong force for near-term social change.

Components of Paradigms

Keeping in mind the several belief structures found in modern societies with respect to these basic beliefs about the relationship between humans and nature, let's return to Table 2.1 to discuss the sharply contrasting beliefs of the vanguard that is pushing for a new environmental paradigm and the rearguard that is defending the old dominant social paradigm.

Valuation on Nature

Previous studies conducted at the Environmental Studies Center at SUNY Buffalo disclosed that one of the outstanding characteristics of environmentalists is their high valuation of nature. Everyone values nature, of course, but environmentalists value it for its own sake; many of them have an almost worshipful love for it. The rearguard also likes nature but they believe a strong emphasis should be given to using nature to produce material goods. One of the items in the three-nation study asked respondents to choose, on a seven-point scale, between a society that emphasizes preserving nature for its own sake in contrast to a society that uses nature to produce the goods we use. Table 2 in Appendix C reports the percentages of each of the samples, in each of the three countries, selecting positions on that seven-point scale.

Both the public and various leadership groups in each of the countries were broadly distributed across all seven categories. The mean score for the public in the United States and England is very close to the middle category while the Germans lean slightly toward preserving nature. People are not experiencing great inner conflict between these two values; if that were the case, there would be high percentages choosing the middle categories. The data show, rather, that people hold widely differing beliefs about the proper relationship between humans and nature.

The environmentalists, many of whom are in the vanguard, and business leaders, many of whom are in the rearguard, display sharply contrasting beliefs with respect to this relationship in all three countries. Nearly all of the environmentalists believe that nature should be preserved for its own sake while business leaders are more likely to emphasize using nature to produce material goods. These widely differing beliefs about the proper relationship between humans and nature are likely to be a continuing area of contention for many years to come; there was very little change from 1980 to 1982.

Economic Growth vs. Environmental Protection

A high valuation on economic growth is a key belief in the old dominant social paradigm; it is highly valued in nearly all countries. When people are simply asked whether or not economic growth is a valuable thing, it is typical for a large proportion to assert that it has a high societal value. People in industrialized countries also value a safe and clean environment. Since the vigorous pursuit of one of these values may diminish realization of the other, it is important to know how people trade off these values when selecting an emphasis for the society that they live in. This tradeoff illustrates the vertical dimension of Figure 2.1. One of the items in our study asked respondents to choose on a seven-point scale whether they would prefer to live in a society that emphasizes environmental protection *over* economic growth or a society that emphasizes economic growth *over* environmental protection. This turned out to be one of the most powerful items in our study for delineating a central belief and value difference between the vanguard proponents of the NEP and the rearguard defenders of the DSP. Table 3 in Appendix C reports the distributions of the various samples in each of the three countries on this item for both 1980 and 1982. There is a great deal of information in that table that I will summarize here.

One would suppose from attending to the media and listening to political discourse that nearly everyone prefers economic growth over environmental protection; that's what the old DSP tells them and the idea is constantly reinforced by leaders in business and government. The data from the three-nation study show, however, that people in the United States chose environmental protection over economic growth by a ratio of 3 to 1 in both 1980 and 1982. The public in Germany also selected environmental protection over economic growth by a ratio of 3 to 1 in 1980 and 2 to 1 in 1982; in England the ratio was nearly 5 to 1. These high ratios in favor of environmental protection were not simply an artifact of question wording or of the use of a mail questionnaire. The Minnesota Poll in the fall of 1981 used a similar question and found the public there selecting environmental protection over economic growth by a ratio of 2.5 to 1. A 7,010-respondent personal interview survey, conducted by the Harris Organization in the fall of 1979, used a question nearly identical to that used in the three-nation study; that study found a ratio in favor of environmental protection of 2 to 1 (see Appendix E).

This question much more strongly differentiates groups within countries than it shows differences across countries. Environmentalists in all three countries were clearly in the vanguard, being nearly unanimous in favor of environmental protection over economic growth. It might be supposed that business leaders would be nearly unanimous in the opposite direction, but that was not the case. Business leaders in all three countries, and in both waves of the study, tended to be undecided when they were requested to choose between these two values; high percentages took a neutral, or near neutral, position (see Table 3 in Appendix C). Labor leaders in England especially favored environmental protection but labor leaders in the United States also leaned in that direction in both 1980 and 1982. A substantial number of the public officials took a neutral position but overall they favored environmental protection over economic growth; the same was true for media gate-keepers in the United States in 1980. This tradeoff seems to be somewhat more divisive among the public in Germany than in England and the United States (this can be seen in both years). Even though the public favors environmental protection over economic growth, the large differences between the rearguard and the vanguard within countries signals that this will be an issue of strong political contention for many years to come.

Despite the contentiousness of the issue, it is an extremely important finding that the broad public, and most leaders, in these countries favor environmental protection over economic growth. This item, probably more than any other, discloses a readiness for developing a new kind of society with a more careful and thoughtful relationship between humans and nature. That is why the major body of the public is sketched in Figure 2.1 as leaning closer to the vanguard than to the rearguard.

When we studied the factors in the U.S. data that differentiated people who took extremes on this question, it was clear that this was the centerpiece in the contrasting belief structures of the old DSP and the new NEP. Some correlates stood out especially strongly. Those people preferring environmental protection over economic growth have an especially strong love of nature; they also believe more strongly that humans are damaging nature, and have a sense of urgency about moving quickly to solve environmental problems. They also strongly emphasize foresight and planning for the public good instead of relying on the market, and they prefer active participation by citizens in governmental decision making rather than leaving those decisions to the leaders in the establishment.

Generalized Compassion

The studies at SUNY Buffalo's Environmental Studies Center, referred to above, disclosed a second important value difference between environmentalists and non-environmentalists. Nearly everyone feels compassion for those that are near and dear; but there are significant differences in degrees of readiness to extend compassion to those more remote from oneself. Environmentalists, much more than non-environmentalists, have a generalized sense of compassion that extends to other species, to people in remote communities and countries, and to future generations. In contrast, the competitive market system of the DSP urges us to look out for ourselves first and to strive mightily to defeat our competitors. Our economic system pressures people in our society to produce and consume at high rates and to give little thought to resources for the future. Is this behavior pattern an accurate reflection of our true values?

One of the items in the three-nation study asked respondents if they would prefer to live in "a country that saves its resources to benefit future generations" or one "that uses its resources to benefit the present generation"; these extremes were again separated by the seven-point scale. The distributions of the various samples on that item are reported in Table 4 in Appendix C. The data show that there was a strong emphasis by people in all three countries on saving resources for future generations. Once again, the environmentalists and the business leaders provide the contrasting emphases (the publics in England and Germany were closer to business leaders than to environmentalists). Nearly half of the environmentalists in the United States and England, and 71% in Germany, were in the most extreme category in favor of saving resources for the future. Business leaders also leaned in that direction but were much less emphatic; German business leaders were more in favor of conserving than American business leaders. The public weights saving for the future four times as heavily as it does gratification in the present. This same item was used in the Harris Survey mentioned above, and showed a very similar response pattern to that of the U.S. public in our sample (see Appendix E).

The sense of compassion for future generations also finds expression in support for the peace movement. Data from the three-nation study, that will be discussed more fully in Chapters 3 and 4, show that many people support both the environmental and peace movements but the overlap is considerably greater in Germany than in the U.S. and England. In Germany, 82% of the environmentalists and 58% of the general public support both movements; 45% of the business leaders oppose both movements. The strongest emotional issue in both movements is opposition to nuclear weapons and nuclear power. The leaders of our German research team believe that these two movements have become the main vehicle for anti-establishment political action in Germany; they are becoming a significant force for revolutionary change. In March, 1983, a political coalition of these two movements known as "the Greens" managed to capture about 25 seats in the German Federal Parliament.

How Should We Handle Risk?

As the people in modern societies struggle to extract resources from the earth to manufacture products that they consume and later discard, they presumably are making a better life for themselves. Unfortunately, we are learning the bitter lesson that as people exuberantly pursue these activities they place themselves, and others, in serious risk of physical injury. Recent revelations of injuries from toxic and hazardous wastes dramatize the problem of risk in modern society. People are beginning to demand that their government adopt policies to protect them from risk or to help alleviate the losses they suffer as a result of exposure to hazard or injury. This raises the question, how much risk should be tolerated in a good society? Nearly all activities involve some level of risk, but what is an appropriate and tolerable level? To what length should society go to control risk as it attempts to produce the goods it needs?

An item in the 1982 questionnaire asked if people would prefer to live in a society that *plans* to avoid physical risks in the production of wealth or one that recognizes that physical risks are unavoidable in the production of wealth. The distributions of our various samples on that item are shown in Table 5 in Appendix C. As with so many other beliefs, the posture that people take toward risk sharply differentiates rearguard from vanguard and business leaders from environmentalists in all three countries. Environmentalists strongly emphasized that society should avoid physical risks in the production of wealth. Business leaders in the U.S. leaned strongly toward accepting physical risks while in England and Germany they were widely spread across the scale having a mean close to the mid-point in the scale. The public in all three countries leaned somewhat more toward avoiding than toward accepting risk but there were wide differences of opinion on this question in all three countries.

When we examined the data to try to discover why some people were risk acceptors and others were risk avoiders, there seemed to be a connection between this posture toward risk and perception of what is going on in the world around one. Those wishing to avoid risk perceived exceptionally high danger from nuclear power. Risk avoiders also had much less faith in science and technology and were, in fact, fearful that technology was running away with society. They also perceived higher levels of damage to nature from the actions of humans. With the exception of environmentalists, gender also played an important role with males more likely to favor risk acceptance while females tended to desire risk avoidance. Interestingly, older people were more accepting of risk than young people.

The DSP, with its exuberant role toward nature in a competitive market system, urges humans to accept risk in order to maximize wealth. The strong defenders of the DSP believe that science and technology have been a great boon to humans and they have a deep and firm faith that swift and continual technological development will continue to be good for humans. This belief is so firmly embedded in modern society, and is given such frequent reinforcement in advertising and public discourse, that the items that we used to measure faith in science and technology (1.3, 1.6, 1.10, 1.14) disclosed overwhelming endorsement for its beneficial effects. Environmentalists, by and large, do not reject science and technology but they have much greater reservations and would proceed with more caution. This was clearly demonstrated by the responses in the U.S. in 1980 to the item, "the good effects of technology outweigh its bad effects." There was strong agreement with this statement among business leaders (83%) and the general public (50%), but much less among environmentalists (32%). For the item, "science and technology are our best hope for the future," 78% of the business leaders and 62% of the public were in the two top categories, but only 38% of the environmentalists strongly agreed with this statement. For the item, "we are in danger of letting technology run away with us," 58% of the business leaders, 24% of the public and only 13% of the environmentalists were in the two highest levels of disagreement.

Most environmentalists were fearful of nuclear power and would like to stop its further development. Defenders of the DSP, on the other hand, generally believe that we should proceed swiftly to develop nuclear power. Turning again to some illustrative items from the 1980 study in the United States, we see that for the item, "the storage of nuclear wastes is too dangerous," 72% of environmentalists along with 49% of the public, but only 17% of the business leaders are in the two top categories of agreement. For the item, "a nuclear accident resulting in the contamination of the environment is increasingly likely," 72% of the environmentalists, 45% of the public but only 16% of the business leaders were in the two top categories of agreement. For the item, "we need nuclear power," 53% of the environmentalists disagreed, but only 19% of the public and 3% of the business leaders disagreed.

Large nuclear power plants are a prime example of "hard" technology. Such plants are massive and intricate technological installations costing several billion dollars. Generally, supporters of the DSP encourage "hard" tech and "high" tech development. The vanguard challengers of the DSP tend to believe that hard and high technology developments are damaging to the biosphere, wasteful of resources, vulnerable to breakdown, and place people at physical risk. Because of these beliefs, they perceive hard-high tech as more likely to enslave people than to free them. They propose, instead, that humans should use their ingenuity to develop "soft" or "appropriate" technology. These technologies are smaller in scale, less complicated to build, less difficult to control, less wasteful of resources, less expensive, less damaging to the biosphere, and, because they decentralize their operations, they are less likely to result in massive disruptive breakdowns. The development of solar energy as an alternative to nuclear energy illustrates these contrasting approaches. Appropriate technology has become the theme of a sub-movement within the overall environmental movement (Morrison, 1980). Many observers who would like to help the less-developed third-world countries to more adequately take care of their material needs, without repeating some of the worst mistakes of the developed countries, are urging the adoption of soft or appropriate technologies as the major developmental thrust of those countries.

The Environmental Protection Agencies that have been set up in more than 100 countries are eloquent testimony to the fact that people look to their government to protect them from physical risks. The market system of the DSP, with its emphasis on individual responsibility to avoid risk, has not provided sufficient protection to satisfy most people. In April, 1983, for example, 58% of the American people agreed that "protecting the environment is so important that requirements and standards cannot be too high and continuing environmental improvements must be made regardless of cost." An item that appeared in the 1982 wave of the three-nation study (but in the U.S. only) asked people if they would prefer to live in "a country where people believe that considerable governmental regulation is required to protect the environment" or in "a country where people believe that little government regulation is required to protect the environment." Governmental regulation was strongly endorsed by the public (66%), even more strongly endorsed by the environmentalists (79%), but less so by business leaders (47%).

Limits to Growth

One of the challenges to the DSP, which we noted in the first chapter, is that the growth in human population and in resource usage is so great that it can't possibly be sustained. This point has been made repeatedly in hundreds of publications and thousands of public meetings in modern industrial countries over the past decade. Whether or not there truly are "limits to growth" continues to be a raging controversy, even today, in most industrialized countries. One of the items in the three-nation study asked respondents the extent of their agreement or disagreement with the item, "There are limits to growth beyond which our industrialized society cannot expand." Figure 2.2 presents the mean score on that item, sample by sample, for each of the countries for 1980 and 1982. It can be seen from the figure that the German people are much more accepting of the idea of limits to growth while the people in the U.S. are most resistant to that idea, with the English people somewhere between the two. The U.S. respondents were widely distributed across the scale; this means that there is strong disagreement about this question in the United States, whereas in Germany, 78% of the public were in the top three categories of agreement and 95% of the environmentalists were in those categories. (Figure 2.2 shows U.S. environmentalists with a lower mean in 1982 than in 1980; this occurred because we deliberately added more "nature conservationists" to our 1982 sample [see Appendix E]; individuals had not changed their views from 1980 to 1982.) The reader can also see in Figure 2.2 that environmentalists were most likely to accept limits to growth and business leaders were most likely to resist the idea, with the public falling somewhere between the two.

The belief that there are limits to growth is related to the belief that there are likely to be resource shortages. The first item on the questionnaire asked respondents if they agreed or disagreed that "there are likely to be serious and disruptive shortages of essential raw materials if things go on as they are." In all three countries, in both years, there

Figure 2.2

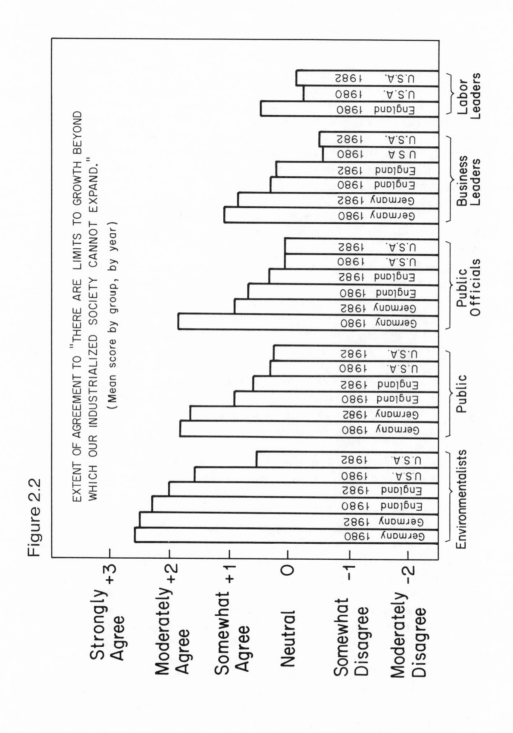

EXTENT OF AGREEMENT TO "THERE ARE LIMITS TO GROWTH BEYOND
WHICH OUR INDUSTRIALIZED SOCIETY CANNOT EXPAND."
(Mean score by group, by year)

was substantial agreement with that view; 65% to 95% of the samples indicated some level of agreement. As usual, environmentalists showed the strongest levels of agreement and business leaders were most likely to disagree.

Much the same pattern of agreement was shown for this item, "We are approaching the limit of the number of people the earth can support." Overall, the extent of agreement was somewhat less than for the resource shortage item; as a matter of fact, about 30% of the American public disagreed with that item in 1982 as compared to 21% in 1980. The people in Germany and England, that experience much greater population densities, are more likely to believe that we are approaching a population growth limit.

When a society experiences an actual shortage, such as the energy shortage of the mid to late 1970's, the way that people propose to deal with that shortage reflects their basic paradigm beliefs. Adherents of the old DSP believe that we should react to such a shortage by vigorously digging out and exploiting the necessary resources to produce the energy. Adherents of the NEP are more likely to adjust to a shortage by reducing their consumption and conserving dwindling supplies. We asked people in the United States to choose whether they would prefer to live in a society that emphasizes conservation or increased production to meet our energy needs. In 1980, 71% of the general public in the U.S. selected a conservation emphasis in contrast to 19% who selected a production emphasis; by 1982, 77% took the conservation emphasis and only 13% the production emphasis (the remainder were in the neutral category). The 1979 Harris Survey used the same question; 59% selected the conservation emphasis and 26% the production emphasis.

As might be expected, environmentalists selected conservation nearly unanimously. Although business leaders in 1980 were widely spread across the spectrum, displaying no pattern of emphasis on this question at all, they selected, in 1982, conservation over production by a ratio of 2 to 1. Labor leaders and public officials fairly strongly favored conservation in both years. It is evident from these data that people in the U.S. view this problem from the perspective of the NEP and that they have a readiness for energy conservation that probably would result in more conserving behavior if appropriate institutional changes could be made that would facilitate the expression of that readiness.

Overall, we see that the people in these three countries have accepted the idea of resource shortages, that there are limits to population growth, and that an appropriate response to shortages is to conserve. In Germany, these beliefs seem to generalize readily to a belief in the limits to growth. In the U.S., however, many people find it very difficult to believe that there are limits to growth. This idea is so contrary to the belief and behavior patterns that have dominated public life in America for 200 years that many people will steadfastly resist the idea until events force them to recognize it. (Of course, they are betting that they will never have to recognize it.)

Do We Need a New Society?

Everyone would agree that there are plenty of things wrong with modern society. The disagreement is centered on whether those flaws are fundamental to the nature of society or whether that society is basically sound and only needs thoughtful reform. Those people who believe that society needs fundamental change haven't agreed upon a blueprint for a superior society but there are some common elements in their critique of the old society and in their beliefs about what would be better.

Humans Seriously Damaging Nature

There is no doubt that modern industrial society inflicts some damage on nature. The defenders of the DSP believe the damage is not serious and can be taken care of by technical fixes whereas the advocates of the NEP believe that the damage is so serious that we must drastically alter our way of doing things. An item asking if mankind is severely abusing the environment showed one of the strongest correlations with an environmentalism scale that we developed for this study (see Appendix D for a listing of the items in the scale). In all three countries, the great proportion of each of our samples agreed with the "mankind severely abusing" item. Environmentalists tended to strongly agree whereas the responses of business leaders were spread widely across the scale; even among them, a majority agreed with the item. In all three countries, 75% or more of the public agreed with the item.

Openness and Participation

In the old DSP, it is widely believed that hierarchical structure, particularly in business firms, leads to efficiency as well as to speedy and wise decisions. The environmental vanguard objects to that kind of decision-making structure because it has so often been used to exploit and injure nature and/or to dominate and possibly injure weak and poor people. This fits with the emphasis of the DSP on material wealth in contrast to the emphasis of the NEP on compassion and protection of nature.

An item in the three-nation study asked people to choose, on a seven-point scale, the extent of their preference for "a society which is willing to put up with some delay in order to let more people have a say in the big decisions" vs. "a society which is willing to let a few people make the big decisions in order to get things done more quickly." In all three countries, there was a strong preference for delaying things in order to let more people have a say but there was a very strong emphasis on this by the environmentalists in contrast to the business leaders who were more likely to want a few people to make the big decisions (their responses were widely distributed across the scale). In all three countries, the public also strongly favored letting people have a say in these decisions. The democratic heritage of the Americans has taught them to value citizen participation in public affairs; Americans much more than the Germans or English are in favor of letting people have a say on big decisions.

This last point is illustrated even more strongly by an item that asked respondents to indicate their preference for "a society with many chances for citizens to take part in political decisions" vs. "a society with few chances for citizens to take part in political decisions." In the United States, overwhelming percentages favored citizens taking part in decisions with 55% or more in the most extreme categories. The samples in England and Germany also leaned in that direction but not so unanimously or so extremely; only the environmentalists in those two countries were sweepingly in favor of participation. In Germany, 30% of the broad public and 42% of the buisness leaders favored a society with few chances for citizens to take part in political decisions.

Public Goods vs. the Market

It is a central tenet of the old DSP that the supply and demand market can be relied upon to allocate resources so as to maximize the public good. A contrasting view insists that we must rely on foresight and planning in order to realize the public good. An item in the 1980 questionnaire asked respondents to indicate their preference for "a society that emphasizes foresight and planning for the public good" vs. "a society that relies on the supply and demand market to maximize the public good." [3] There was a clear tendency in England and the United States for respondents to prefer foresight and planning over the market (unfortunately, the German translation used the phrase "central planning," making that item not truly comparable to the English language version). Labor leaders and environmentalists in both England and the U.S. distinctively displayed a strong preference for foresight and planning. The public, interestingly, also placed a strong emphasis on foresight and planning. Business leaders in both countries were most likely to favor using the supply and demand market but they were far from unanimous in this position. As a matter of fact, U.S. business leaders were strongly split on this question with some business leaders strongly favoring the market while others strongly favored foresight and planning. Business leaders in England, in contrast to those in the United States, were mostly undecided (took middle positions on the scale) in trying to select between these two emphases for society.

When we decided to repeat this item on the 1982 questionnaire, we also decided to make explicit what we thought had been implicit in the 1980 wording. The new wording read, "emphasizes foresight and planning *by government* for the public good." This seemingly innocent wording change produced a large shift in the response pattern of U.S. respondents in 1982. Public responses were now almost evenly divided between planning and the market although there continued to be a tendency for people to take extreme positions on the issue. Environmentalists who had been sweepingly in favor of planning when responding to the 1980 version of the question now had 25% favoring the market. Business leaders who had been sharply divided in 1980 now were in substantial agreement in favor of the market. Labor leaders, curiously, were almost as strongly in favor of planning in 1982 as they had been in 1980. Equally interesting, but not so surprising, was the finding that elected officials were now more in favor of planning, but appointed officials showed little change.

The English respondents also shifted toward the market when responding to the 1982 version of the question but not as sharply as U.S. respondents. All groups, with the exception of business leaders who were fairly evenly spread across the scale, continued to favor planning despite the insertion of *government* into the wording.

In Germany, where they continued in 1982 to use the item with the phrasing "central planning," the public, business leaders and members of Parliament were overwhelmingly opposed to central planning in both years of the study. The environmentalists, curiously, were spread widely across the scale with a mean close to the center.

It seems clear from these findings that the words "planning," "government," and "market" trigger strong reactions causing many people to take extreme positions on this question. These views seem clearly to be part of two differing social paradigms with people on the opposite ends of the scale generally partaking in the cluster of beliefs that go with the respective paradigms we have been discussing. No matter which wording of the item, we found the now familiar patterns of the environmental vanguard leaning distinctively in the direction of foresight and planning as contrasted with the business leaders who were distinctively leaning in favor of the market. Many of the items that we have discussed so far in this book have shown little relationship to left-right political ideology, but we found for this item that liberals and Democrats were more likely to favor foresight and planning whereas conservatives and Republicans were more likely to favor the market.

Another item, that was used only in the U.S. study, asked respondents to choose between a society that emphasizes using taxes to insure that public goods (parks, clean air, recreation facilities, etc.) are well provided and a society that minimizes taxes, paying individuals maximum personal incomes. In 1980 all groups, with the exception of business leaders, strongly favored using taxes to insure provision of these public goods. Even business leaders leaned in that direction but their responses were quite scattered across the scale. That basic response pattern held also in the 1982 study even though Ronald Reagan had been elected president in the interim on a platform of minimizing taxes and deemphasizing public goods.

Competition vs. Cooperation

There are elements of both cooperation and competition in the relationships among people in nearly all societies. But does society work better if one or the other emphasis is predominant? The rearguard defenders of the DSP assert that society benefits when people compete vigorously with one another. The NEP challengers assert that society works best if people cooperate rather than compete.

In the U.S. component of the three-nation study, the American samples were asked (this question was not used in England and Germany) if they preferred to live in a country that emphasizes competition or a country that emphasizes cooperation. Among the general public the preference for cooperation was even stronger in 1982 than it was in 1980 at a ratio of better than 2 to 1. Environmentalists displayed a sweepingly strong preference for cooperation in contrast to business leaders who showed a nearly equally strong preference for competition in 1980. By 1982, business leaders had moved somewhat toward co-operation while environmentalists continued to be nearly unanimous in preference for cooperation. In 1980, labor leaders strongly endorsed cooperation over competition and they had moved even more decisively in that direction by 1982. Public officials slightly emphasized cooperation in 1980 and moved somewhat further in that direction in 1982. The evidence is clear in the U.S. that very many people have departed from the DSP emphasis on competition as the best way of structuring relationships between people.

Lifestyles

Beliefs about the proper structure for society carry over to preferences for lifestyles. Adherents of the DSP, with its belief that humans should take an exuberant dominating role toward nature, are likely to prefer to live complex and fast lifestyles. Modern day advertising urges people to "live life in the fast lane." A beer commercial suggests that "since we only go around once in life, we should do it with gusto." Advocates of the NEP believe that exuberant and dominating postures toward nature will not only injure the biosphere but also are likely to diminish quality of life; they urge simple lifestyles with more contemplative pleasures.

An item used only in the U.S. study asked if an effective long-range solution of environmental problems depends upon "changing our life-style" or "developing better technology" (the two alternatives were separated by a seven-point scale). Environmentalists overwhelmingly believed that a solution would require a change in lifestyle, whereas business leaders overwhelmingly looked to development of better tech-nology. The U.S. public, in 1980, had responses that were widely distributed across the scale but, curiously, there was a tendency to take extreme positions on each end of the scale. When the item was repeated in 1982, these extreme preferences were toned down a bit and the responses were distributed fairly evenly across all seven positions on the scale. Labor leaders leaned fairly strongly towards better technology but a substantial minority favored changing lifestyles.

The Meaning of Work

Defenders of the DSP, with its emphasis on economic values and material wealth, view employment as a means to obtain material goods and they believe in organizing work so as to maximize productive output. The challengers to the DSP argue that work ought to be satisfying in its own right; that fulfillment in the work setting is an important component of high quality of life.

An item in the three-nation study asked for the extent of preference people had for "a society which emphasizes work which is humanly satisfying" vs. "a society where work is controlled mainly by economic needs." In all three countries, for both years, there was a strong preference for a society that emphasizes work which is humanly satisfying. The by-now-familiar differences between elites appear on this item as well; environmentalists were in the vanguard urging work which is humanly satisfying and business leaders' responses spread across the scale with a substantial proportion of them preferring a society where work is controlled mainly by economic needs. Union leaders were nearly as strongly in favor of work which is humanly satisfying as were environmentalists.

Post-Materialism

A group of people who elevate non-material values are referred to by many social scientists as "post-materialists"; Inglehart (1971, 1977, 1981, 1982) is the leading analyst of "post-materialist" values. This is not the place for a thorough discussion of the theory of post-materialism nor of the findings from a large number of studies. Many of the beliefs and values identified here as characteristic of the NEP also characterize the post-materialists: protection of the environment, compassion toward other people, openness and participation in public affairs, high quality but simple lifestyles, and emphasis on jobs that are humanly satisfying. A cluster of 12 items that Inglehart used to measure post-materialism were included on the questionnaire in the English study (see Appendix D). They showed that environmentalists and advocates of the NEP were considerably more likely to be post-materialists than the average person in the sample.

New Politics

Persons who advocate a new belief structure for a new society inevitably urge a new politics. The impact of environmentalists on politics will be discussed in Chapter 5 of this book. Suffice it to say here that in the NEP perspective, politics should be consultative and participatory whereas defenders of the DSP believe that many political decisions should mainly be determined by experts. We saw above that advocates of the NEP believe that foresight and planning are essential to protection of the biosphere and for the provision of public goods while DSP defenders believe that market mechanisms are adequate for that task. Our data also show that most people in the vanguard are willing to use direct action tactics such as demonstrations, protests, and boycotts in order to try to get their messages to be heard by public decision makers. Defenders of the DSP are quite strongly opposed to direct action and believe that all participants should use normal channels for communication (which DSP adherents believe are adequate but NEP supporters believe are inaccessible to persons with their point of view).

Politics has, for many decades now, been organized along a left-right axis where the main dispute between political parties is over the ownership of the means of production. The advocates of the NEP feel that capitalism vs. socialism is no longer the major dispute in modern society; that it is much more relevant to devote their energies to finding a more satisfactory relationship between humans and nature. As they push strongly for a new and more satisfactory relationship between humans and nature, they are likely to be opposed by the rearguard defenders of the DSP. These clashing viewpoints have the *potential* to shift party contesting away from the old left-right axis to a new axis, as sketched above in Figure 2.1. We also should expect that left-right contending will continue in many places. Some day we may see a merger of the NEP with a new "ecological Marxism" (Agger, 1979, Ch. 7).

The political aspects of the NEP vs. DSP clash of paradigms will be more fully discussed in Chapter 5.

Summary

A variety of findings from the three-nation study have been introduced to provide empirical evidence in support of the distinctions summarized in Table 2.1. In addition to demonstrating that each of these two belief structures are cohesive and quite contrasting, the findings also show that there is substantial movement away from the DSP toward the NEP, at least at the level of beliefs and values, even among some business leaders. This shift is not yet fully reflected in behavior and it is not yet widely recognized by people who report on and/or discuss public affairs. For reasons mentioned in the last section of the first chapter, we should expect this lag to exist.

NOTES

1. The point just made is valid for most contemporary governments. It does not apply to all Marxists, however. The neo-Hegelian-Marxist group that

draws on 1844 Marx believes that nature should be valued; see Leiss (1974).

2. Michael Marien (1982) also postulates that politics is developing a new second axis. Additionally, he compares the contrasting visions for two types of post-industrial societies.

3. It is conceivable that some respondents did not perceive this scale, or others, as polar opposites. Foresight and planning are possible in a society that also uses markets. This item is not intended as a choice between capitalism and socialism; rather respondents are asked for a preferred emphasis for their society.

THREE

Portrait of a Revolution in Process

Paradigms are structures of beliefs in people's minds. Such beliefs cannot be directly sensed or measured, they can only be inferred. An analysis will be presented in this chapter that supports the inferences and interpretations advanced previously in this book. It was worked out conceptually by the German and American teams in the three-nation study.[1] This analysis should help to persuade the reader that in each of these three modern industrial countries there is a rearguard defense of the DSP that is being seriously challenged by vanguard reformers, mainly environmentalists. It will show the opposing beliefs of these two groups and how those beliefs cluster into paradigm-like structures. The analysis also will show that most of the public in these countries fall somewhere between these two contending elites and that within this larger group there also are unique clusters of beliefs. The analysis will show how these belief clusters are distributed within the public and also within the various elite samples of our studies.

Three Key Beliefs that Distinguish Vanguard from Rearguard

An initial exploration, mainly conducted by Fietkau and Coopersmith, identified three variables that strikingly separated people and that, very likely, were key concepts, in paradigm shift. They reasoned that if we could divide up the sample according to these three variables, we could most clearly identify the psychological, social and political dynamics involved in the social change we were studying.

Awareness and Concern

Over the past two decades there has been a growing awareness of environmental problems that has created a high level of concern about the best way for society to deal with them. This has become a strong psychological thrust pressuring for social change. The single best item that measures this phenomenon in this study reads, "I perceive the condition of the world environment as: no problem vs. large problem"; the two extremes are separated by a seven-point scale. Hardly anyone perceived the condition of the environment as no problem; therefore, in dividing the sample into two parts, those responding in categories 6 and 7 were classified as perceiving a large problem and those responding in categories 1–5 were classified as perceiving a small problem.

Basic Change vs. Technological Development

The way that people perceive the environmental problem shapes their beliefs about appropriate solutions. One of the most powerful items in this study asked, "What kind of change is most needed to solve our environmental problems? Greater scientific and technical development or basic change in the nature of society? " The alternatives were separated by a seven-point scale. The full distributions on this scale for each of our samples are shown in Table 6 in Appendix C. In each of the countries, people took widely differing and extreme positions on this issue. As suggested in Chapter 2, this belief should sharply differentiate rearguard from vanguard; the environmentalists took strong positions in favor of basic change and business leaders took strong positions in favor of scientific and technical development. In dividing up the samples on this variable, the respondents taking the middle category, expressing no preference for the alternatives, were eliminated from the analysis so as to more sharply delineate the types we were deriving.

Limits to Growth

The concept of limits to growth, that was discussed in Chapter 2, also was identified as a key concept for differentiating the beliefs of people. Again, the holders of the middle position on this dimension were dropped from the analysis to more sharply delineate the types.

As can be seen schematically at the top of Tables 3.1, 3.2 and 3.3, the sample was first divided as to whether people thought the environmental problem was large or small. Next it was divided as to whether people thought it could be solved by better technology or would require a basic change in society. Finally, it was divided as to whether or not people believed there are limits to growth. The resulting 8 types are numbered across the bottom of the tables. We began this analysis expecting to look at a variety of demographic, value, and belief variables to describe the kinds of people that fell in each of these 8 types. As the analysis proceeded, however, we were somewhat astonished to discover that we had, in fact, created a powerful variable for measuring postures toward social change. If the types are arranged in the logical structure shown in the Tables, and the resulting dimension is cross-classified with other variables, we discovered, again and again, that there was a neat linear progression from left to right across the dimension.[2]

It seems clear from the analyses already discussed in Chapter 2 that people who believe the environmental problem is small, that it can be solved by technical fixes, and that there are no limits to growth should be labeled rearguard; this belief structure fits squarely within the DSP. At the opposite extreme, those who believe that the environmental problem is large, that it can be solved only by basic change in society, and that there are limits to growth should be labeled vanguard; that belief structure clearly is within the NEP. Persons who perceive a large environmental problem but who opt for technological development rather that basic social change to solve it are labeled nature conservationists. The other derived types will be discussed later in the chapter.

A tremendous amount of information is presented in Tables 3.1, 3.2, and 3.3; they may initially appear to be overwhelming but patient study will disclose that there is a significant advantage in having all of this information brought together on single pages. We will first study the horizontal rows across the tables and later study the vertical columns to develop verbal portraits of each type. This analysis was conducted with the entire file, including all the leadership groups as well as the public in each country. This not only provides more cases for analysis, but also shows where the elites are located in this struggle for social change. Table 3.1 includes data from the United States for 1980 and 1982; this will enable us to make some modest comparisons over time. Because the German and English teams did not include the item on better technology vs. social change in their 1980 study, the data reported in Table 3.2 for Germany and 3.3 for England are confined to 1982.

Postures Toward Social Change

The meaning of the typology can most clearly be shown by studying its relationship to the variables that measure postures toward social change. If the conceptual structure set forth in Figure 2.1 and Table 2.1 is approximately correct, these variables will distribute along the main axis of conflict separating vanguard from rearguard.

Should One Change Parties?

Respondents were asked to estimate the probability that they would be influenced in their choice of party at the next election by its policy on environmental questions. The percentage of people reporting they probably would change parties in that circumstance ascends in a nearly linear fashion as we scan across the tables from Type 1 to Type 8. In the United States, in 1980, only eight or nine percent of the people on the left side of the table indicated they would probably change but 43% on the right side indicated they probably would do so. By 1982, those percentages had risen dramatically in each of the types; Type 8 had climbed to 68%.

The Germans and English, in 1982, showed a pattern with a similarly steep ascendency across the types. The Pearson correlation coefficient (r) expresses the strength of this relationship;[3] in the U.S. it was .38 in 1980, and .43 in 1982. In England it was .46 and in Germany it was .40.

In comparing Germany with the United States and England, the reader should keep in mind that Germany already has developed "Green" ecology parties (Borklin, 1981; Capra and Spretnak, 1984) but this has

TABLE 3.1
Types of Actors in Social Change
(Portrait of a Revolution in Process)
U.S. Sample 1980 and 1982

Column group structure:

- **Small Problem**
  - *Better Technology* — no limits: **Rearguard**; yes, limits: **Establishment**
  - *Basic Change in Society* — no limits: **Weakly Active Est. Followers**; yes, limits: **Undecided Middle**
- **Large Problem**
  - *Better Technology* — no limits: **Nature Cons. Establish. Followers**; yes, limits: **Nature Conservationists**
  - *Basic Change in Society* — no limits: **Young, lower Class Env. Sympathizers**; yes, limits: **Vanguard**

(Row headers above the data: Perceived Condition of Environment / Change Most Needed to Solve Environmental Problems / Are There Limits to Growth? / Type Name / Year)

Type Name →	Rearguard		Establishment		Weakly Active Est. Followers		Undecided Middle		Nature Cons. Establish. Followers		Nature Conservationists		Young, lower Class Env. Sympathizers		Vanguard	
Year	80	82	80	82	80	82	80	82	80	82	80	82	80	82	80	82
Percent-of Whole file	21	20	14	10	10	10	16	18	5	5	7	7	7	6	21	24
Percent-of Public	18	17	14	9	11	14	19	26	5	4	8	6	8	5	18	19
Postures toward Change																
Percent-Probably Change Parties	9	15	8	14	4	11	12	18	6	33	10	50	8	46	43	68
Mean-Support Direct Action	2.29	2.24	2.53	2.34	2.71	2.99	3.29	3.20	3.24		3.92	4.15	4.01	4.57	4.56	5.11
Mean-Support Peace Movement		2.52		2.70		3.07		3.44		3.98		4.16		4.60		5.41
Percent-Join Environmental Group	17	23	22	31	24	22	24	35	25	41	35	56	37	46	54	72
Percent-Mean Active on Env. Issues	17	2.85	22	2.61	17	2.31	27	2.75	30	2.90	28	3.77	31	3.29	48	3.79
Percent-Complained About Env. Problem		41		41		38		48		47		71		57		78
Mean-Need for Nuclear Power	6.10	5.81	5.90	5.26	5.37	5.09	5.18	4.34	5.76	4.56	5.00	4.21	4.54	3.55	3.79	2.61
Mean-Planning vs. Market	3.83	4.61	3.52	4.61	3.20	4.19	3.02	3.93	3.06	3.73	2.56	3.34	2.31	3.23	2.41	2.82
Mean-Preserve Nature vs. Produce Goods	4.82	5.13	4.56	4.27	4.38	4.27	4.06	3.98	3.97	3.65	4.04	3.51	3.59	3.31	2.71	2.74
Mean-Avoid vs. Recognize Risks		4.52		4.36		3.70		3.53		3.27		3.52		2.65		2.56
Mean-Env. Protection vs. Econ. Growth	4.12	4.45	3.76	4.11	3.57	3.76	3.03	3.02	2.87	3.00	2.56	2.34	2.30	2.36	1.94	1.87
Respondent's Perceived Influence																
Mean-Perception Environmental Influence	3.24		3.40	4.65	3.16	4.49	3.05	4.77	3.56	4.82	3.38	5.16	3.24	4.65	3.74	5.08
Mean-Perception Influence Locally		3.29		2.97		3.14		3.03		2.61		3.06		2.36		3.09
Mean-Perception Influence Nationally		2.72		2.54		2.49		2.46		2.24		2.75		2.17		2.78
Distribution of Leaders																
Percent-Business Leaders	48	45	20	21	6	9	11	10	5	7	4	1	1	5	3	3
Percent-Labor Leaders	25	24	15	10	16	9	5	14	8	8	8	9	10	12	13	14
Percent-Appointed Officials	26	23	15	16	12	11	17	14	6	8	5	9	6	5	14	14
Percent-Elected Officials	24	22	16	16	18	13	18	16	6	6	2	6	2	0	22	22
Percent-Environmentalists	4	6	2	2	3	2	6	10	2	2	6	11	6	5	71	62
Percent-Media Gatekeepers	22		25		9		6		3		6		3		25	
Demographics																
Percent-in Service Sector	29	30	32	38	48	39	46	57	47	37	45	64	54	54	59	76
Sex: Percent Male	81	89	78	79	66	67	59	60	71	75	74	77	50	55	57	59
Education	high		high		medium		low		medium		medium		low		high	
Income	high		high		medium		low		medium		medium		low		med. high	
Age	medium		older		medium		medium		older		older		younger		young	
Number	348	203	229	105	165	103	260	183	78	49	112	69	108	58	351	250
Type	1		2		3		4		5		6		7		8	

TABLE 3.2
Types of Actors in Social Change
(Portrait of a Revolution in Process)
German Sample 1982

Perceived Condition of Environment	Small Problem				Large Problem			
Change most needed to Solve Environmental Problems	Better Technology		Basic Change in Society		Better Technology		Basic Change in Society	
Are There Limits to Growth?	no limits	yes, limits	no limits	yes, limits	no limits	yes, limits	no limits	yes, limits
Type Name	Rearguard	Establish-ment	Weakly Active Est. Followers	Undecided Middle	Nature Cons. Establish. Followers	Nature Conserva-tionists	Young, lower Class Env. Sym-pathizers	Vanguard
Postures toward Change								
Percent of Whole file	6	23	1	12	3	18	2	34
Percent of Public	5	24	1	15	3	20	2	29
Percent-Probably Change Parties	8	9	6	15	13	34	29	50
Mean-Support Direct Action	1.95	2.47	3.12	3.41	3.74	4.37	4.83	5.63
Mean-Support Peace Movement	2.44	3.14	3.75	4.05	4.15	4.89	5.52	6.01
Percent-Join Environmental Groups	19	15	12	13	24	31	38	47
Mean-Activity on Env. Issues	3.38	3.49	3.29	3.25	4.41	4.16	4.38	4.68
Percent-Complained on Env. Problem	18	23	29	22	33	38	36	54
Mean-Need for Nuclear Power	6.39	5.90	5.47	4.98	5.47	4.67	3.31	2.81
Mean-Planning vs. Market	6.42	5.68	4.24	4.99	4.71	5.44	4.76	4.56
Mean-Preserve Nature vs. Produce Goods	4.51	3.98	4.24	3.51	3.41	3.26	3.86	2.99
Mean-Avoid vs. Accept Risks	4.15	3.36	3.94	3.45	2.85	3.02	3.07	2.56
Mean-Env. Protection vs. Econ. Growth	4.36	3.74	3.76	3.25	3.16	3.10	4.03	2.48
Respondent's Perceived Influence								
Mean-Perception Environmental Influence	3.52	3.14	2.94	3.01	3.76	3.32	3.31	3.16
Mean-Perception Local Influence	3.11	2.54	2.47	2.27	3.21	2.50	2.45	2.52
Mean-Perception National Influence	2.57	2.11	2.00	2.04	2.70	2.05	1.72	1.90
Distribution of Leaders								
Percent-Business Leaders	23	52	3	8	1	9	0	5
Percent-Members of Parliament	16	27	1	18	5	9	1	22
Percent-Environmentalists	1	3	0	1	1	17	3	74
Demographics								
Percent-Service Sector	22	33	33	51	33	44	58	56
Percent-Male	81	71	59	53	76	56	72	62
Education	high	medium	medium	low	medium	low	medium	high
Income	high	high	high	medium	medium	low	low	low
Mean Age	42	47	46	41	36	46	36	38
Number	85	307	17	165	34	242	29	458
Type	1	2	3	4	5	6	7	8

TABLE 3.3
Types of Actors in Social Change
(Portrait of a Revolution in Process)
English Sample 1982

Perceived Condition of Environment	Small Problem				Large Problem			
Change most needed to Solve Environmental Problems	Better Technology		Basic Change in Society		Better Technology		Basic Change in Society	
Are There Limits to Growth?	no limits	yes, limits	no limits	yes, limits	no limits	yes, limits	no limits	yes, limits
Type Name	Rearguard	Establishment	Weakly Active Est. Followers	Undecided Middle	Nature Cons. Establish. Followers	Nature Conservationists	Young, lower Class Env. Sympathizers	Vanguard
Percent of Whole file	12	11	11	21	1	4	5	35
Percent of Public	9	14	19	25	2	3	5	24
Postures toward Change								
Percent-Probably Change Parties	4	8	7	18	25	24	26	53
Mean-Support Direct Action	2.67	3.00	3.01	3.17	3.58	3.90	3.72	5.10
Mean-Support Peace Movement	2.73	2.95	3.40	3.62	3.58	4.29	4.42	5.37
Percent-Join Environmental Groups	22	25	18	34	33	57	49	77
Mean-Activity on Env. Issues	2.31	2.22	2.22	2.37	3.08	2.74	2.92	3.62
Percent-Complained on Env. Problem	42	43	40	46	75	53	56	88
Mean-Need for Nuclear Power	5.55	5.42	4.75	4.59	5.42	4.81	4.00	2.84
Mean-Planning vs. Market	4.53	3.64	3.57	3.21	3.33	2.74	3.24	2.50
Mean-Preserve Nature vs. Produce	4.97	4.25	4.12	4.01	3.25	3.48	3.17	2.84
Mean-Avoid vs. Accept Risks	4.55	3.86	3.63	3.63	2.58	3.10	2.93	2.49
Mean-Env. Protection vs. Econ. Growth	4.30	3.49	3.16	2.81	2.83	2.48	2.19	1.62
Respondents Perceived Influence								
Mean-Perception Environmental Influence	4.26	4.22	3.91	4.31	4.33	3.84	4.56	4.13
Mean-Perception Local Influence	2.48	2.15	2.03	2.13	2.17	2.58	2.33	2.26
Mean-Perception National Influence	2.36	1.79	1.81	1.98	2.09	2.29	1.81	1.86
Distribution of Leaders								
Percent-Business Leaders	25	19	14	27	2	2	4	7
Percent-Public Officials	20	11	5	24	2	7	13	18
Percent-Environmentalists	1	4	4	13	1	4	2	72
Demographics								
Percent-Service Sector	34	27	35	43	27	73	47	62
Percent-Male	87	83	69	75	83	73	77	60
Education	high	medium	low	medium	low	high	low	high
Income	high	high	low	med./high	medium	medium	med./high	low
Mean Age	47	49	47	48	52	48	46	49
Number	101	99	96	185	12	31	43	310
Type	1	2	3	4	5	6	7	8

not occurred in England and the U.S.. Part of the relationship shown in Table 3.2. for probability of changing parties in Germany was contributed by persons who already identify with Green parties; nearly all of them fall in Type 6 and 8 and nearly all have already changed parties. When the Greens are removed from the Table, the correlation falls to .30. Many of the Greens are former Social Democrats (SPD). Those hard-core SPD identifiers who had not left the fold, as a matter of fact, were less inclined than the rest of the population to change parties because of environmental policy. The most recent evidence from Germany, prior to publication, shows that the SPD leaders, who lost the March 1983 election, are now moving closer to the Greens, especially with respect to nuclear power and nuclear weapons.

Direct Action

In all three countries, people were quite divided over whether or not it is good for society when groups use direct actions such as protests, demonstrations and boycotts as a means of expressing their grievances and viewpoints. Such actions have become quite common in all three countries in the late 70's and early 80's. Generally, the established leadership (that already has good access) opposes the use of direct action whereas groups lacking normal channels of influence tend to favor the use of direct action. Respondents were simply asked to respond on a seven point scale whether they favored or opposed the use of direct action. Scanning across on the tables discloses that support for direct action ascended nearly linearly from Type 1 to Type 8 in all three countries and, in the United States, for both years. The Pearson correlation rose from .43 in 1980 in the U.S. to .54 in 1982; this is one of several indicators that, on these social change issues, conflict is sharpening in the United States between the rearguard and the vanguard. The German data showed a similarly sharply ascending order from rearguard to vanguard, (Pearson r = .59). The ascendency in the English data was a less dramatic .44.

The Peace Movement

The peace movement has been active throughout the decades since World War II but it blossomed forth with considerable strength in Europe in the late 70's and early 80's, and in the U.S. in 1982, enlisting many hundreds of thousands in public demonstrations in favor of peace, disarmament, a nuclear weapons freeze, etc. As mentioned above, there is a natural affinity between the environmental movement and the peace movement; both movements are based on strong compassion for others and both constitute strong thrusts toward social change.

An item simply asking, on a seven point scale, if people favored or opposed the peace movement showed support ascending linearly as we read across the tables from rearguard to vanguard. The Pearson r for the U.S. was .52, for Germany it was .54, and in England it was .46.

As mentioned above, the relationship between the two movements was especially strong in Germany with 58% of the public and 82% of the environmentalists favoring both while 45% of the business leaders opposed both. In the U.S., the relationship between the two movements was not so strong; only 21% of the public favored both movements, 15% opposed both and 64% had mixed responses. Much of the same was true for England where 29% of the public favored both, 11% opposed both and the remainder were mixed. Among American environmentalists, 63% favored both, 4% opposed both, whereas among U.S. business leaders, 13% favored both and 35% opposed both.

Joining Environmental Groups

Joining a group generally is seen as an effective way to help insure that one's voice is heard with respect to public issues. Group activity requires some skills and entails some costs in time and money; studies generally have shown that persons of high income and education are better able to bear these costs. This consideration affects distribution of the percentages of persons joining environmental groups in the various types. The people in both the rearguard and the vanguard are better educated and have higher incomes than the average person and also are of a more activist nature. Because of this, we find 20 to 30% of Types 1 and 2 belonging to environmental groups. As expected, there is a clear rise in the percentage of joiners as we scan across from rearguard to vanguard.

The table shows that the percentage joining groups in the U.S. was higher in 1982 than in 1980. There was a slight wording change in 1982 that picked up past memberships as well as current memberships but this wording change, alone, does not account for the increase in group membership in 1982. Many U.S. environmental groups have reported recent increases in membership and attribute this to the threat to the environment that people perceive from the Reagan administration. It seems likely that many of these new members have been drawn from the leadership strata, however. The "whole file" used for this analysis contains a higher ratio of elites in 1982 than in 1980. When the proportion joining environmental groups is examined for the public only, the increases are modest.

The question used in 1982 was identical in all three countries and shows significantly higher group participation in the U.S. than in Germany (with England falling between the two). This is a true cultural difference in that group activity is a more common form of political participation in the U.S. than in Germany. The question used in 1982 also showed that about 45% of the public in the U.S., 55% in England and 60% in Germany were interested in becoming members of environmental groups; this is a vast untapped potential. It is of special interest that so many Germans are interested in environmental groups despite their cultural tradition of not joining groups. The environmental issue seems to have special mobilizing power; more Germans now belong to environmental groups than belong to political parties.[4]

In England, a distinction can quite clearly be drawn between members of nature conservation groups who typically are oriented to preserving beautiful nature, but are fairly conservative politically and resist social change, and members of environmental groups that typically seek more fundamental social change. This distinction is less clearcut in the United States where many of the former conservation groups have become transformed into environmental groups (see Chapter 4 for further development of this). We asked about membership in each of these types of groups on both questionnaires. Cross-tabulation of the two questions, each year, enabled us to separate the sample into four categories:

1) Those who belonged to both types of groups.
2) Those who belonged to environmental groups only.
3) Those who belonged to nature conservation groups only.
4) Those who were not members of either type of group.

Percentages falling in each of these categories, for each of the types delineated in the rearguard-vanguard dimension, are reported in Table 3.4 for the U.S. in 1980 and 1982, and for Germany and England in 1982. The persons in the vanguard tend to belong to both kinds of groups while the persons in the rearguard tend to belong to neither kind of group; if they do join a group, it is much more likely to be a nature conservation association than an environmental group. If persons in the vanguard don't belong to both types of groups, they are more likely to be in environmental groups. Persons in Types 5 and 6, who perceive a large environmental problem but believe it can be solved by better technology rather than by social change, are more likely to join nature conservation groups than environmental groups. The reader should keep in mind that we only asked about joining environmental groups; naturally, many of the people in the rearguard would not be attracted to such groups.

Environmental Activity

Although we asked about activity on environmental issues in both studies, the items were somewhat different; hence, the findings from 1980 cannot strictly be compared to 1982. The question asked about activity on environmental issues and did not ask about the direction of that activity; some may have been active trying to dilute environmental protection while others were trying to strengthen it. Scanning across the tables, we can see that the most active people tended to be found toward the extremes of the rearguard-vanguard dimension with much higher activity levels toward the vanguard end of the scale.

TABLE 3.4
Percentage Joining Environmental Groups
By Types on the Rearguard-Vanguard Dimension

	Rearguard						Vanguard	
	1	2	3	4	5	6	7	8
				U.S. 80				
Both types of groups	7	8	9	9	9	13	22	37
Environmental groups only	3	5	4	7	7	10	7.5	11
Nature conservation groups only	7	9	11	8	9	12	7.5	6
Neither	82	78	77	76	75	65	63	46
				U.S. 82				
Both types of groups	12	11	11	16	25	45	30	60
Environmental groups only	2	4	4	4	4	2	4	8
Nature conservation groups only	9	16	7	15	12	9	12	4
Neither	77	69	78	65	59	45	54	28
				Germany 82				
Both types of groups	4	3	0	1	3	13	21	29
Environmental groups only	1	2	6	4	9	6	10	9
Nature conservation groups only	13	11	6	8	12	12	7	9
Neither	82	85	88	87	76	69	62	53
				England 82				
Both types of groups	5	9	7	17	25	29	21	54
Environmental groups only	1	2	1	2	0	7	3	9
Nature conservation groups only	16	13	11	15	8	21	26	14
Neither	78	75	82	66	67	43	51	23

Lodging Complaints

We also asked people if they had complained to someone in authority about environmental problems. Substantial percentages reported having complained in the United States and England with slightly lower percentages in Germany. Although it is clear tht the people on the vanguard end of the dimension were much more likely to lodge such complaints than people in the rearguard, there was not a clean linear progression from rearguard to vanguard; persons in Type 6 in the U.S. were significantly more likely to complain than persons in Type 7, for example.

Nuclear Power

As discussed above, beliefs about the wisdom of developing nuclear power have been very divisive between the rearguard and the vanguard. Respondents were asked to judge the need for nuclear power on a seven-point scale and the means for each type are reported in the tables; they disclose that there is a declining support for nuclear power that is almost linear as we read across from Type 1 to Type 8. The one exception, which holds for all three countries, is the group in Type 5 that recognizes that the environment is a large problem, would solve it through better technology, and also denies limits to growth; one can understand that this group would more strongly favor nuclear power. The Pearson r expressing the strength of the relationship between responses to this item and the rearguard-vanguard dimension was .40 for the U.S. in 1980 but rose to .53 for the U.S. in 1982, .45 for England in 1982, and .57 for Germany in 1982.[5]

Note also that in the United States there was less support in 1982 than in 1980 for nuclear power, in all eight types. This same shift was shown in responses to items 1.2 and 1.5 in the respective years, reflecting an increase in fear of nuclear power over the two year period; the change on these items was not as great, however, as for the item measuring need for nuclear power. Since Tables 3.1, 3.2, and 3.3 deal with the whole file, we checked to see if the change in support for nuclear power held for the public alone. The decline in support for nuclear power was slightly greater among the public than it was among the elite in all three countries. This shift is not attributable to sampling error; approximately half of the people in the U.S. public sample in 1982 were the identical persons who responded to the 1980 questionnaire; the loss in support for nuclear power was of the same magnitude for the previous respondents as it was for the new respondents. We can speculate that this loss is related to the sharply rising concern about nuclear war, as well as increasing support for a nuclear freeze and disarmament that has been evident in these three countries recently. Our data, however do not contain appropriate questions to provide conclusive evidence supporting this supposition.

Planning vs. Market

The emphasis of the NEP vanguard on foresight and planning and the emphasis of the rearguard on using the market to allocate goods and services were discussed above in Chapter 2; recall that the two words "by government" were added to the 1982 version of the question. No matter which version of the question is used, the means reported in Tables 3.1, 3.2, and 3.3 disclose a strong relationship between the rearguard-vanguard dimension and this item. In contrast to some of the previously examined items, however, the progression is not linear from type to type. Generally this is because persons in Type 5 who are in favor of better technology and perceive no limits to growth are more likely to favor the market.

The Human Relationship to Nature

The item asking people if they would prefer a society that emphasizes preserving nature for its own sake vs. a society that emphasizes using nature to produce the goods we use was discussed above in Chapter 2. The mean scores on this item for each of the types on the rearguard to vanguard dimension are reported in the tables and confirm that this is an important philosophical difference between the rearguard and the vanguard.

Acceptability of Risk

Persons who are willing to exploit nature to produce goods generally are more willing to accept physical risks in order to produce greater wealth. The means shown in Table 3.1 disclose that the willingness to accept physical risk declines nearly linearly from rearguard to vanguard. A similar decline also was observable in the German and English samples but they were not quite so linear as in the U.S. The decline also was not as steep on this issue as on some of those previously discussed. This is because environmentalists themselves are divided on this issue. Typically, environmentalists are nearly unanimous in taking a fairly extreme position on many of these items, but on the question of risk, although they lean in the direction of planning to avoid risk, there are many who believe that society must accept some unavoidable risks.

Economic Growth vs. Environmental Protection

The reader will recall from the discussion in Chapter 2 that most people value economic growth *and* environmental protection; therefore, it is necessary to trade off the two values in order to find out which is perceived to be more important. Reading Tables 3.1, 3.2, and 3.3 it is clear that the rearguard prefers economic growth to environmental protection whereas the vanguard prefers the opposite. In all three countries, the decline is nearly linear from rearguard to vanguard. In the United States, the Pearson correlation expressing the strength of the relationship was .45 in 1980 and .55 in 1982; conflict on this issue apparently sharpened over the two-year period.

Perceptions of Influence

We asked respondents, "How much influence do you have as a result of your own efforts and activities, over the following areas of your daily life?"; they rated their influence on a seven-point scale running from "little" to "much." The mean levels of perceived influence on local political decisions, regional and national political decisions and on environmental decisions at place of residence are reported in Tables 3.1, 3.2, and 3.3. Generally, the rearguard *and* the vanguard in the U.S. and Germany had the highest perceived influence on all three questions (Type 6 in the U.S. and Type 5 in Germany were the exceptions). The Americans generally perceived higher levels of influence than did Germans; this was especially true for influence on the local environment. Perceptions of influence were not clearly related to the rearguard-vanguard dimension in England. Note that the vanguard in both Germany and England perceives itself as having little *political* influence.

Descriptions of Types on the Rearguard-Vanguard Dimension

The findings presented so far probably are sufficient to give the reader a sense of the strong differences in belief between the rearguard and the vanguard. The remaining data in these tables are more readily examined by reading down the columns for each of the types. As we decriptively delineate the types, the data sets from all three countries will be drawn on to profile each type.

The Rearguard

Type 1, the rearguard, constituted 18% of the U.S. public in the 1980 sample and 17% in 1982. The percentage of the whole file appearing in this type was somewhat larger, reflecting the fact that a high proportion of the elites also fall in this type. This can be seen by reading further down the column which shows that nearly half of the U.S. business leaders fall into this type as well as about a fourth of the labor leaders, media gatekeepers, appointed officials, and elected officials. In the United States, it is clear that the rearguard is made up of many powerful people.

These persons are predominantly male and tend to have high income and education. In terms of age, they are near the middle of the distribution. Most importantly, they have a low percentage of people employed in the service sector; meaning that most of them are employed in the production sector. To make this comparison, we took our question on "sector of employment" (item 6.5) and combined the various categories of people working in the production sector and, similarly, combined categories of people working in the service sector (this excluded some respondents from the analysis who do not fall clearly in either sector). The percentage reported in the table can be read as a ratio of people employed in the production sector compared to those employed in the service sector. The reported percentages in the service sector rise nearly linearly as we read across from rearguard to vanguard.

The service sector is growing in numbers and importance, particularly in Germany but also in the U.S. and England. Note in the U.S. table there was a rise in the proportion of people in the service sector within each type as we compare 1980 with 1982. This rise was particularly strong for those who selected limits to growth rather than no limits. Only people in Type 5 showed a decline in the percentage in the service sector from 1980 and 1982; these people believe in better technology and no limits to growth but do recognize a large environmental problem. These environmentally-aware people still seem to be deeply embedded in the values and beliefs of the production sector. All in all, we should expect that, if the American economy continues to transform from a production to a service emphasis, there will be further growth in the vanguard. These data suggest that sector of employment has a profound influence on perceptions, values, and beliefs about how the world works.

Type 1 in the German and English samples is demographically very similar to Type 1 in the U.S. sample; their beliefs also are similar. The main difference between the countries is that only 5% of the public in

Germany and 9% in England fall in this category as contrasted to 17% in the U.S.; this is because a larger portion of the English and especially the German people believe that there are limits to growth. That also is why 52% of the German business leaders and 27% of the members of the German Parliament are found in the second rather than the first type. In that country, in many respects, they are the rearguard.

The Establishment

The description of Type 2 will begin with the profile from Germany. This type incorporates approximately a quarter of the German public, a majority of the business leaders and more than a fourth of the members of Parliament, but very few environmentalists. The Type 2 group is somewhat older than Type 1 and has a slightly higher proportion in the service sector. On most belief and value items it is typically less extreme than the group in Type 1.

The Type 2 group in the U.S. and England is similar demographically to Type 2 in Germany. It has a slightly higher proportion of males than in Germany; this is mainly because the public (that sample includes more females) constitutes a smaller proportion of this group in the U.S. and England than it does in Germany. As a matter of fact, the proportion of the U.S. public falling in this type dropped from 14% in 1980 to 9% in 1982. Where did these people go? Probably into Types 3 and 4 that show substantial increases in the percentage of the public falling in them from 1980 to 1982; this increase can be traced to a larger portion of the public believing in 1982 that environmental problems can only be solved by basic social change. The reader will note that substantial proportions of the leadership groups (except environmentalists) fall into Type 2. For all of these reasons, then, they are labeled "the establishment."

Weakly Active Establishment Followers

The main distinction between Type 3 and the previous two types is that this group more likely recognizes the need for a basic change in society. It was difficult to come up with a simple name for them; we finally settled on "weakly active establishment followers." They are not very active in public affairs and have low perceptions of their political influence. Demographically they are not very distinctive either, falling near the median on most variables in the U.S. and Germany. In the U.S., they constitute 11% to 14% of the public, but in Germany this group, that denies limits to growth, makes up only 1% of the public. In England, this type had 19% of the public. The people in this type tend to be of low education and income and a comparatively high proportion of them are females. On most belief and value items, these persons are appropriately placed as Type 3 on the rearguard-vanguard dimension, that is, leaning more to the rearguard than to the vanguard.

Undecided Middle

Type 4 is an interesting group. Its members want a basic change in society and they also perceive limits to growth but they do not regard the environmental problem as a large problem. They tend to be low in income and education in the U.S. but are at medium levels in England and Germany; they also are medium in age. They are composed of an unusually high proportion of service workers; about half or more of them are in the service sector (this may help to explain why they perceive the need for basic change and limits to growth even though they are less ecologically aware). In the U.S. and England in 1982, a larger proportion of the public fell in Type 4 than in any other, which explains why this type has a larger proportion of females than most other types. In Germany, this type has only about 15% of the public in it; this is probably because a larger proportion of the German public than the U.S. and English publics perceive the environment to be a large problem; this perception would move them into Types 6 and 8. In Germany, 18% of the members of Parliament are in this type as well as 8% of the business leaders. In England, about a quarter of the business leaders and public officials are found here. In the U.S., this type also has a sizable representation of leadership groups, particularly appointed and elected officials.

It is useful to reflect on the particular combination of beliefs represented by this type. They believe that there are limits to growth and that a basic change is needed in society in order to solve environmental problems; yet they do not perceive the condition of the environment to be a large problem. This suggests that disenchantment with the DSP is taking place in these people even though they are not particularly environmentally aware. Departure from the DSP can occur for many reasons; not all of these people will respond to the vanguard trying to lead them to a new environmental paradigm.

Nature Conservationist Establishment Followers

The people in Type 5 perceive a large environmental problem that they believe can be solved by better technology and they do not perceive limits to growth. In many respects they are like the rearguard, the main difference is that they perceive the environment to be a considerably larger problem than is perceived by the rearguard. About a quarter of them in the U.S. 1982 sample belong to both environmental and nature conservation groups. People in this type also value material wealth fairly strongly and most of them wish to preserve the present form of society. For these reasons, we have named this type "nature conservationist establishment followers."

The people in Type 5 constitute only about 5% of the U.S. public, 3% of the German public, and only 2% of the English public. The percentages probably are small here because the belief pattern is somewhat anomalous; it is unusual for technology enthusiasts who deny limits to growth also to believe there is a large environmental problem. In philosophical perspective, they are very similar to the rearguard.

For the above reasons, I am reluctant to treat this type very seriously; a substantial proportion of them could have fallen here as a result of misunderstanding the questions or because of hasty response. Note that only 12 persons fall in this type in the English sample. For all of these considerations, I will forego drawing a demographic profile of this type.

Nature Conservationists

In Figure 2.1, we define nature conservationists as persons who strongly advocate environmental protection but who do not desire basic social change. As defined in the tables in this chapter, these people believe that there is a large environmental problem and that there are limits to growth but they believe better technology is preferable to basic social change for resolving environmental problems. They constitute 6 to 8% of the public in the United States, 3% in England, and 20% in Germany. A comparatively high proportion of these people belong to environmental groups. In the U.S. and England, they generally belong to both environmental and nature conservation groups; if they belong to only one kind, it is likely to be a nature conservation group (see Table 3.4). A high proportion (50% in the U.S., 34% in Germany, and 24% in England in 1982) indicate that they would be willing to change parties because of the environmental stances of the parties.

In the United States, people in Type 6 tend to be medium in education and income; in England they are high in education and medium in income; in Germany, they tend to be low on these two measures (this may be because substantial proportions of the public fall in this type in Germany). In both Germany and the U.S., this type is a little older than the average but they are average in England. A fairly high percentage of people in this type are employed in the service sector in England and the United States; this percentage increased in the U.S. from 45% in 1980 to 64% in 1982. The percentage in Germany was 44. In the United States and England, about three-fourths of this type are males, but in Germany the male percentage is only 56, probably because this type incorporates many of the public. Many of the nature conservationists in the United States love hunting and fishing; the fact that these sports predominantly attract males may account for the high proportion of males in this type in the U.S.

In the United States, nature conservationists perceive that they have quite a lot of influence on local environmental policy but only moderate influence on other local political problems or on national problems. In Germany, probably because of the high proportion of the public in this type, the perceptions of influence are lower. In England, the nature conservationists perceive that they have low influence on local environmental policy but greater influence than other types on local and national policy.

Young, Lower Class, Environmental Sympathizers

Type 7 is another anomalous type; these people perceive a large environmental problem and the need for basic change in society but they do not believe there are limits to growth. In Germany, where very few believe there are no limits to growth, this combination classifies only 2% of the population but in the United States and England, 5 to 8% of the public are classified here. This group is not as inclined to change parties as persons in Type 6 in the U.S. and Germany; party change is clearly linked to belief in limits to growth in those countries.

In the U.S., this type has the lowest income and education, they tend to be young, and they have the highest percentage of females of any type. Of the elites, only labor leaders have a substantial representation here. In England, their education level is low but income is medium to high; nearly three-fourths of them are male, and as in the U.S., they tend to be young. A substantial proportion of public officials fall in this type. Type 7 in Germany has a low income level but their education level is medium; three-fourths of them tend to be males and they are young. Relatively few elites fall in this type.

The anomalous belief structure and the peculiar demographic characteristics shown for this type in the various countries made this group hard to understand; we shall be exploring the data further to try to unravel the puzzle. We speculate that, being young, this group has the environmental sympathies of its contemporaries. Being disadvantaged, they would like to see basic social change. Being poorly educated, they probably do not see the rationale for limits to growth and, furthermore, they may look to economic growth to improve their situation.

The Vanguard

Type 8 is much easier to summarize; the people here perceive a large environmental problem, they want basic social change to solve it and they perceive that there are limits to growth. On nearly every belief and value dimension, this type was in the most extreme position challenging the rearguard. They are seeking a fundamental redirection for society and can be named the vanguard.

It is surprising that a relatively high proportion of the public fall into this classification, 18–19% in the United States, 24% in England and 29% in Germany. Perhaps even more significantly, there is a high representation of leaders in the vanguard. Only 3 to 7% of the business leaders fall here but 13 to 25% of the other leadership groups in the U.S. study are part of the vanguard; in Germany, 22% of the members of Parliament are in this group and in England, 18% of public officials are in this type. Not surprisingly, two-thirds to three-fourths of the environmentalists are found in this group. The percentage of environmentalists in the vanguard in the U.S. was 71% in 1980 but only 62% in the 1982 sample. This change occurred because we supplemented our environmental sample in 1982 with more nature conservationists.

That change also explains why the percentage of environmentalists in Type 6 rose from 6 in 1980 to 11 in 1982 and those in Type 4 increased from 6 to 10.

Nearly three-fourths of the vanguard in the U.S. and England had joined environmental groups; in Germany, nearly half had done so. A high percentage of the vanguard also indicated they probably would change parties at the next election because of party stances on environmental issues. There were substantial increases on both of these measures within the U.S. vanguard from 1980 to 1982; this suggests a slowly increasing militancy and a sharpening of political conflict with the rearguard. The vanguard in the U.S. perceives that it has high influence on local environmental questions and a moderate ability to influence other local and national policies. The vanguard in England and Germany perceives that it has substantially lower ability to influence policies, ranking near the bottom of all types.

The vanguard has an exceptionally high proportion of its members working in the service sector; in the U.S. vanguard, there was a 17% jump in service employment from 1980 to 1982. In all three countries, the vanguard incorporates a substantial proportion of females. This accords with findings from a number of studies that women are more attracted to environmentalism than men (for a summary of citations, see Chapter 4). The vanguard also is comparatively young (except in England). They have the highest level of education of any of the types but have substantially lower incomes (keep in mind there are many women in this group), being among the lowest in Germany and England, and only medium high in the United States.

Careful study of all of the characteristics of the vanguard in all three countries suggests that this type constitutes a powerful potential for social change. We detect that their numbers are slowly increasing, partly due to conversion to their beliefs and partly due to demographic changes such as the dying off of the somewhat older rearguard and the conversion of modern economies from production to service employment. A number of findings from this as well as other studies show that many of the public share the views of the vanguard. Our data also show that substantial numbers of various leadership groups are part of the vanguard. Although the rearguard continues to dominate politics and governance in each of these countries, the vanguard may soon be in a position to successfully challenge it. In Germany's recent federal election (March 1983), the "Green Parties" were unsuccessful in their attempt to prevent CDS party leader, Helmut Kohl, from retaining the position of Chancellor, but they did manage to obtain about 25 seats in the Parliament. In the U.S. and England, persons of this persuasion lack a common political rallying point to aggregate their influence and make it felt effectively.

Discussion

The tables we have just examined reveal almost a classic portrait of the dynamic forces involved in revolutionary but peaceful social change. A vanguard perceives that the old system is no longer working and begins to cohere around a new philosophy that people perceive to be superior to the old DSP. This group tends to be young and well educated; as such it is likely to possess the enthusiasm and ego strength to believe that it can move the people to accept a new social system. As this group becomes active politically and in educating the public, it slowly succeeds in gaining adherents and in acquiring political power.

The rearguard defenders of the DSP undoubtedly will recognize this challenge to their dominant position and they are likely to coalesce their forces so as to provide more effective opposition. The rearguard currently has a large proportion of the elites agreeing with its philosophy, but the data also show that there has been substantial erosion of support away from the DSP, even among the elites.

Substantial proportions of the public agree strongly with the views of either the rearguard or the vanguard. The bulk of the public, however, holds a combination of beliefs that lie somewhere between them. The German public seems to have moved a bit further toward the vanguard than seems to be the case in the U.S. and England, but even in Germany it probably will take some time before the vanguard acquires sufficient supporters and a sufficiently effective political organization to be able to successfully battle the rearguard for political domination in the country. In the U.S. and in England, the day when the vanguard might successfully challenge the rearguard seems far in the future.

It might be helpful to close this chapter with a recapitulation of the things we have learned from our study.

Overall Conclusions

1) The three items dealing with perceived size of the environmental problem, type of change most needed to solve it, and whether or not there are limits to growth can be divided and subdivided into eight types that distribute remarkably well along a rearguard to vanguard dimension.
2) The large number of highly significant differences between rearguard and vanguard (many more could have been added but the tables were overfull as is) demonstrates the reality of sharp divisions over these fundamental beliefs in modern society.
   a) These sharp divisions on fundamentals imply continued conflict for some time to come.
3) The fact that so many variables correlated so highly with the rearguard-vanguard dimension, and that there are high inter-

correlations among these variables, demonstrates the cohesiveness of the vanguard and rearguard belief structures. They are paradigms that tell their adherents how the world works.

Comparisons Across Types

1) Most business leaders and substantial proportions of labor leaders, public officials, and media gatekeepers are adherents of the rearguard.
2) While we expected to find environmentalists strongly represented in the vanguard, it was surprising to find a substantial minority of the other leadership groups there as well.
3) Nearly 20% of the U.S. public agrees with the rearguard and 20% with the vanguard but most of the public falls near the middle of the dimension between the two polarized groups. In England, 24% of the public is with the vanguard as contrasted to 9% in the rearguard; most of the public is in the middle between the two poles, however. In Germany, about 30% of the public are found on each end of the dimension. These kinds of questions were not asked in previous studies so we do not know if these proportions have changed from previous decades; we guess that there is an on-going shift from rearguard to vanguard.
4) The rearguard is dominated by people active in the production section of the economy that is oriented toward using market mechanisms for choosing societal direction.
5) The vanguard is largely made up of people active in the service sector of the economy; this group clearly has less economic stake in the preservation of the old DSP.
    a) As industrial economies become oriented more toward service, we can expect the ranks of the vanguard to grow.
6) The rearguard is almost totally dominated by males, whereas the vanguard has a substantial representation of females.
7) Both groups have high education but the rearguard has substantially higher income than the vanguard.
8) The vanguard is much younger than the rearguard (except in England).
    a) Since people tend to retain beliefs developed in their formative years, we can expect, as a pure function of demographics, a shift from rearguard to vanguard as the older rearguard dies sooner.
9) The rearguard perceives itself to be more influential than is reported by other groups while the vanguard sees itself as fairly influential on environmental questions but not very influential on the broad range of local and national problems.

Comparisons Across Countries

1) The Germans seem substantially more environmentally oriented than the Americans; this is especially evident in their nearly unanimous acceptance of limits to growth. Whether or not there are limits to growth continues to be a sharply dividing issue in the United States. England falls between Germany and the U.S. on environmental awareness and concern.

2) A somewhat greater percentage of Americans than Germans or English indicate they would be willing to change political parties because of the environmental stances of those parties; this is particularly true when comparing respondents in the 1982 study. The percentage of Americans ready to change in 1982 also is higher than in 1980.

3) Americans are more likely than Germans to join groups; the proportions joining environmental groups are significantly higher in the U.S. than in Germany for each of the eight types on the rearguard to vanguard dimension. The English, once more, fall between the Germans and Americans.

4) Comparing reported activity levels on environmental issues, the means are consistently higher in Germany than in the United States or England.

5) Americans and English are more likely to complain about environmental problems than are Germans.

6) Americans generally perceive themselves as having higher levels of influence on environmental issues, local issues, and national issues than do the counterpart groupings in Germany and England.

Comparisons Across Time

1) There was a perceptible sharpening of conflict among Americans when comparing 1980 to 1982. This can be observed in the increasing readiness to change parties, in the increased correlation with direct action, in the increased percentage joining environmental groups, and in the increased correlation with the tradeoff between economic growth and environmental protection.

2) There was a detectible movement toward accepting basic social change in the U.S. from 1980 to 1982; this was found among business leaders and labor leaders as well as the public. Public officials showed little change, however.

3) There was a noticeable decline in the perceived need for nuclear power from 1980 to 1982. This drop can be observed in each of the eight types of the rearguard-vanguard dimension in Table 3.1. Similar declines were found in Germany and England.

We make the point early in the chapter that social change must begin in the minds of people. We have shown that people's beliefs about how the world works are undergoing transition in modern developed countries; that the people in the vanguard have quite a different worldview than the people in the rearguard. This worldview serves the values of the vanguard but these people also feel that their beliefs are grounded in reality as to how the world works physically, socially, economically, and politically. In the next two chapters we will discuss the opportunities and the difficulties for expressing these views influentially in the political arena.

We can anticipate that these contrasting worldviews of the rearguard and the vanguard will be in sharp contention in modern industrial societies for many years to come. Eventually it *may* come to pass that the worldview of the vanguard will become the dominant social paradigm just as the old paradigm of the rearguard once became dominant. No one can predict that eventuality with certainty. The data presented here support the possibility of that eventuality; they also suggest that we have progressed a good deal further down the path than one could know from attending to the mass media and listening to the politicians. It seems that the people in modern industrial societies are working their own revolution with very little guidance from political philosophers and very little leadership in the form of a tightly-knit leadership cadre. Revolutions in people's minds work rather quietly but inexorably.

NOTES

1. I am especially indebted to Hans Joachim Fietkau and Hans Kessel of the German team and Jeffrey Coopersmith of the American team for their collaborative efforts in working out the conceptualization and analysis presented in this chapter.

2. The three variables had been selected because of wide differences of response within the public as well as sharp differences between environmentalists and business leaders. They were ordered for analysis by the logical structure we perceived among them. Of course, different ordering, or different variables, could have been used. After seeing how remarkably well *this* ordering of *these three* variables worked, we did, in fact, try other orderings and other variables (about a dozen trials in all). They all "worked" but none worked as well as the ordering we had arrived at prior to beginning data analysis. The story told by the data was the same no matter which combination we examined.

3. We are aware that our data do not meet the assumption of equality of intervals on which the Pearson r is based; it is still the best estimate of the "real" relationship. Non-parametric correlation estimates also were consulted for these and subsequent tables; the story was always the same no matter which coefficient was consulted.

4. Feist and Liepelt (1982) attribute this mobilization partly to post World War II educational reforms that have created a highly educated young middle class that engages in "critical discourse"; this is a sharp departure from traditional German reactions to authority.
5. Environmentalist opposition to nuclear power in Germany demonstrated its political clout in Hamburg, a former bastion of the SPD, in 1980–81. A governmentally sponsored nuclear power plant proposed for Hamburg was vigorously opposed in large noisy demonstrations. The SPD was so split on the nuclear plant issue that it could not take a position; a short while later it lost the state elections for the first time in 30 years.

FOUR

The Environmental Movement

If problems in our present society are to be solved by social change, people must not only recognize the problems and believe that something should be done; they must begin to do things to facilitate that change. But what should they do? If they perceive that there must be basic change in society, as many of them do, they might well flinch from the thought of trying to turn a whole society around. Social change seldom occurs as the result of such grandiose planning.

Most people approach the question "What can I do?" at a more practical level. Usually, they turn to the government to try to get new laws passed, to get officials to enforce existing laws and regulations, to get new officials in office who are more favorable to their viewpoint, to get officials to make better decisions, and try to educate others to join in their efforts. As a matter of fact, helping people to become more aware, better informed, more broadly concerned, more integrative, more creative in problem-solving, and more willing to take sustained action is the very essence of social change; it slowly takes place in people's minds. It is social learning.

People who have already gone through the transformation and are persuaded of the need to help others to make it, too, typically organize a group so as to coordinate their efforts, sustain their enthusiasm, and maximize their effectiveness. Environmentalists have formed thousands of such groups that, taken collectively, have formed into a social movement. It has been estimated, based on requests to the U.S. Internal Revenue Service for tax exemptions, that there are about 12,000 environmental and conservation groups in the U.S.; approximately 250 new ones are organized each year. This social movement already has had considerable impact on the way we do things in modern society (new laws, new processes, new concepts) and, in my judgement, is destined to have an even greater impact in the future.

As with most social movements (Banks, 1972; Ryan, 1969), the environmental movement has undergone some transformation with time (O'Riordan, 1979; McConnell, 1971; Mitchell, 1979b, 1980a; Sandbach, 1980; Faich and Gale, 1971). The modern-day environmental movement has its roots in a conservation movement that achieved some prominence in the late nineteenth and early twentieth centuries in the United States (McConnell, 1954). The plentiful supply of cheap land in the new world led many immigrant settlers to exploit land ruthlessly, with little concern for future generations. Land was treated as a commodity, enabling some people to get rich quickly; this also led to widespread speculation in land ownership. The exploitive mentality toward land was carried to such an extreme that it created a reaction that took the form of the Conservation Movement. One prominent objective of the movement was to set aside certain beautiful tracts of public land as national parks to avoid their being purchased and exploited for private gain. Yellowstone National Park, established in 1872, was the first national park in the world and set a model for park development in the United States as well as in many other countries. The Conservation Movement, led by such famous leaders as Theodore Roosevelt and Gifford Pinchot, had the preservation of beautiful nature as its most prominent objective; this objective continues to be central to the environmental movement today (Pierce, 1979).

Similar conservation movements were getting underway in other countries, most prominently in England, with a similar emphasis on the preservation of unspoiled nature (O'Riordan, 1979; Zetterberg, 1978). Cotgrove (1982, p. 2) has listed 12 British organizations with this objective that were founded either in the last half of the nineteenth century or the first half of the twentieth century. These groups were interested in the preservation of commons, open spaces, footpaths, birds, forests, ancient buildings and monuments, and soils.

A second emphasis for many of the conservationists was efficiency; they perceived waste and despoliation as inefficient and detracting from the ability of society to create wealth (Schnaiberg, 1980, pp. 378–389; O'Riordan, 1971; Hays, 1959). Schnaiberg (1980) sees the efficiency emphasis of the Conservation Movement as strongly supportive of industrial capitalism and the upper middle class. The Conservation Movement was seen by many scholars as upper middle class (Harry, Gale and Hendee, 1969; Devall, 1970a). It is especially important to note that most of the people in the Conservation Movement accepted the existing economic-social-political arrangements of the society; they had excellent access to major economic and political decision makers and did not question the belief and value structure and societal arrangements that dominated this industrially-oriented and market-controlled society. Most of them saw no conflict between conservation and economic growth. Some scholars referred to this group as "Wise Multiple Use Progressives" (Hays, 1959; Nash, 1967).

Another early conservation leader, John Muir, had a different vision of the relationship between humans and nature. He saw man immersed in nature rather than the lord over nature (Devall, 1982; Fox, 1981; Nash, 1967). "Everything is flowing into everything else." His philosophy was deeply spiritual and he became spiritual godfather to later leaders such as Aldo Leopold, Rachel Carson, David Brower, and David Ehrenfeld. He is also godfather to today's "deep ecologists".

As the Conservation Movement grew, it was joined by many people who were interested in such outdoor sports as hunting and fishing. These activities had, and continue to have, attraction for working class persons. Such American groups as the National Rifle Association, and the National Wildlife Federation have hundreds of thousands of members, even millions, and are able to wield considerable influence in public affairs and legislation. Their base has become so broad that they no longer can be called a middle-class movement.

As human degradation of the environment advanced to what many began to believe was an alarming level, the movement began transforming from a conservation movement to an environmental protection movement (Morrison, 1972; Bartell & St. George, 1974). Frightening increases in air and water pollution appeared in the 1960's and were the most visible mobilizing factors (Dillman and Christenson, 1975; Kromm, Probald and Wall, 1973); media attention, such as the focus on the Santa Barbara oil spill of 1968, was particularly significant in focusing public awareness of these problems (Murch, 1971). Awareness of pollution dangers grew swiftly in all classes but was further advanced in the middle class (Buttel and Flinn, 1974). Urban areas, where the degradation was greater, became aware faster and the awareness was more widespread (Erskine, 1972a, 1972b; Tremblay and Dunlap, 1978). Earth Day 1970 was the high point of public consciousness and clamor for environmental clean up.

Many commentators during the 60's also were successful in focusing public attention on problems of population growth; people began to see the connection between increasingly dense population and increasing levels of pollution (Barnett, 1973, 1974; Simon, 1971). Curiously, there was little public understanding during the 1960's of the possibility of resource depletion and the energy shortage that would confront them with a jolt in the 1970's (Milbrath, 1975). Not only were people largely uninformed about possible resource shortages, but they resisted accepting information about them (Bartell, 1976; Jackson, 1980; Anderson and Lipsey, 1978), possibly because a recognition of resource shortages would be likely to require acknowledgement that there would be limits to growth. As we have seen, the idea of limits is very difficult for Americans to accept but is more readily accepted in Germany. The undeniable existence of shortages in the 1970's has slowly eroded that resistance in the U.S. In the latter part of the 1970's, the horrors of toxic waste poisoning began to emerge in a variety of places and a sense of urgency to control toxic wastes soon took a prominent place on the agenda of concerns of the Environmental Movement.

Beginning in the late 60's and continuing into the present, environmentalists have urged people to question proposed technological "advances." Technology can bring evil as well as good. Furthermore, the thrust for ever higher levels of technology can, in many cases, be so inappropriate as to be counterproductive, and even dangerous. This charge was particularly salient for exports of "Western" technology to less developed countries. Highly sophisticated technology may displace workers rather than produce jobs; it is likely to be highly consumptive of energy and other resources; and it is vulnerable to breakdown due to lack of parts and skilled technicians. Environmentalists urged the use of "appropriate" technology, that which is suited to the socio-economic-political realities of a setting. This thrust became something of a mini-social movement with its own networks of interested people and its own literature (Lovins, 1977; Schumacher, 1973; Morrison, 1980). Appropriate technology became one of the important components of the belief structure of environmentalists (Mitchell, 1980a).

Fear of nuclear power intensified and spread widely through the population of industrial societies over the decade of the 70's and continues to increase into the 1980's (Mitchell, 1980c, 1981, 1982). It has become the most emotional and divisive of the environmental concerns. Believers in industrial capitalism could accept the fact that there was air and water pollution and that it was necessary to make vigorous technological efforts to clean it up; they could recognize that population growth is a problem; they could recognize resource shortages and pledge vigorous efforts to find new sources of energy and materials; they could not deny the clamor of the public to be free from toxic poisons and they accepted stiff regulations as well as clean-up campaigns. But the demand of noisy environmentalists to stop further growth and development of nuclear power was perceived as striking at the very heart of modern industrial capitalism. Environmental activists who had found the doors of public offices open to them when they complained about pollution or toxics found a deaf ear and a vigorous determination to plunge ahead when they complained about nuclear power (Slovic, and others, 1982; Nelkin and Pollak, 1980, 1981). Feeling that all other avenues were being closed to them, some environmentalists took to the streets and demonstrated their convictions about nuclear power by throwing their bodies before bulldozers and trucks or chaining themselves to fences, in eloquent evidence of the depth of their feelings.

Fear of nuclear power seems to be linked to fear of nuclear war and fear of technology running wild. People who admire and have faith in technology are much more likely to accept nuclear power (Benedict and others, 1980). As mentioned earlier, there is at present in most advanced industrial societies a linkage between the environmental movement and the peace movement; this is particularly strong in Germany where over half the population favors both movements and 82% of environmentalists see themselves as strong supporters of the peace movement. In 1982, several important environmental organizations in the United States announced that they were taking up studies and campaigns for the purpose of avoiding nuclear war, because such a war would be the most devastating of environmental catastrophes.

Throughout the 1960's and 1970's, awareness developed that environmental problems could not be solved by technological fixes, that solving these problems would require basic changes in society (Milbrath, 1975a, 1981c, 1981d). Awareness of continued population growth, and increasing shortages of raw materials and energy, led many people to conclude that there are limits to growth (Bowman, 1977; Milbrath, 1981d; Cotgrove, 1982). It would be necessary not only to limit growth in human population but also to limit the exuberant way that humans act toward nature. Increasing numbers of environmentalists began to recognize that in order to effectively deal with the problems they saw, they had to challenge the very foundations of modern industrial society. "The environmentalist movement has been forced to change from a consensual to a conflictual movement, from a concern with reform within a framework of consensual values ·· a radical challenge to societal values. The change from a norm-oriented to a value-oriented movement." (Cotgrove, 1982, p. 10).

In Germany, the environmentalists could not get adequate recognition of their views within the traditional party structure and have formed new "Green Parties" that successfully obtained representation in state parliaments as well as the national parliament. In the United States, most environmental organizations have thus far tried to appeal simultaneously to nature conservationists and to reform environmentalists; these two basic kinds of environmentists have worked together for many common goals. The determination of the Reagan administration to turn the nation away from environmentalism and refocus it on economic values has galvanized many national environmental organizations to take overt political action and try to get candidates elected to public office that are favorable to their perspective. Several of these organizations set up political action committees and were happy to report to their members that approximately 70% of the candidates that they supported were successful in winning election in 1982.

Members of the environmental movement, then, while agreed on the importance of protecting the natural environment, are split on whether or not major socio-economic-political change is required in order to have a good society. The reform environmentalists, the vanguard, are proposing a new environmentally-oriented societal paradigm that challenges the old dominant social paradigm defended by the rearguard. The nature conservationists seem to be less certain about their social purpose and partake of both sets of values (paradigms).

It is often asserted that environmentalism is on the decline, that the movement peaked with Earth Day 1970 and has diminished in importance as economic concerns have become increasingly urgent (Schnaiberg, 1980; Dunlap and Van Liere, 1977; Dunlap and Dillman, 1976; Honnold and Nelson, 1981). Is this true? It is helpful to disaggregate the inquiry.

Economic concerns clearly have become more urgent since 1970; even environmentalists give them first rank in urgency (Milbrath, 1981b). The people who claim the primacy of economic values over environmental values, the "rearguard," captured the U.S. Presidency in 1980. The politicians devote less attention to the environment and this depresses media coverage; recently, however, media coverage of environmental degradation has been extensive in the United States. Many environmental laws have been passed and many people feel they are working well (Mitchell, 1980b); this diminishes the clamor for change.

On the other hand, concern about environmental protection and values continues as high as ever (Mitchell, 1978, 1979a, 1980b; Milbrath, 1981a, 1981b; Althoff and Grieg, 1977; Bowman, 1977; Utrup, 1978; Table C-1 in this book). The range of environmental things to be concerned about keeps growing (energy, toxics, nuclear, land use, resource depletion). Fear of nuclear energy is growing (Mitchell, 1980c, 1981, 1982). The Reagan administration's deemphasis of environmental values and proposed weakening of environmental laws have raised a public outcry and swelled memberships in environmental organizations. Both a Harris poll and a New York Times/CBS poll in early 1983 showed a significant increase from 1981 in the percentage of Americans desiring to *strengthen* environmental protection. During 1983 Ann Burford and James Watt, who headed the most environmentally relevant agencies in the Reagan Administration, were both forced to resign; public opinion forced a change in Reagan's environmental policies (Mitchell, 1984). The new values and concerns of environmentalism seem to have taken root and have become a permanent aspect of public life in modern industrial societies. In short, while urgency for environmental protection has taken a back seat to urgency about the economy, environmental concern still remains high.

I recently presented a graduate seminar on "Environmentalism as a Social Movement." Our study group examined numerous articles and books with respect to the movement (see in particular the April, 1980, issue of the *Natural Resources Journal,* Vol. 20, #2 that has a symposium on "Whither Environmentalism? "). At the conclusion of our deliberations we were able to arrive at the following generalizations with respect to the environmental movement:

1) It is a value-oriented reformist movement, but we must make a distinction between environmentalists who wish to retain the present socio-economic-political system and those who wish to drastically change it. Environmental organizations typically try to appeal to both types.

2) The movement is viewed sympathetically by a high percentage of the general public (in the range of 60 to 80%) in most developed industrial countries of the West. There is less awareness and there are fewer sympathizers in eastern European countries and in less developed countries.

3) The movement is well institutionalized in the West and has been sufficiently successful to generate considerable opposition (mostly defenders of the DSP). There are many voluntary organizations that make up the movement with formal memberships running into hundreds of thousands, even millions. In Germany more people belong to environmental organizations than to political parties.

   These organizations are large enough to have their own bureaucracies and lobbyists and are able to have significant impact on legislation as well as on the decisions in public bureaucracies.

4) Most of the organizations that make up the movement have a democratic system for selecting leadership. As with most organizations, leadership tends to be oligarchic with some rotation of leadership over the years (Devall, 1970b).

5) The leadership seems exceptionally dedicated to its cause with many of the leaders working for poor salaries; they tend to be well educated and not charismatic or fanatic. The leadership tends to be drawn from the upper-middle and upper classes (as is true of most organizations) but general membership of the organizations spreads across the full spectrum of socio-economic status.

6) Members are recruited either by direct mail or by proselytizing from person to person. Perception of environmental threat is a prominent motive for joining as is the desire to be out in nature together with others with similar interests.

7) Perception of dire threat from an environmental insult, such as the discovery of toxic waste in a neighborhood, can galvanize formerly unaware and inactive persons to form a new organization and take many kinds of political action. Most of these groups are local, focusing on their immediate problem. Many hundreds of such groups have been formed in the past few years. Some of the participants become transformed to permanent environmental activists (Shaw & Milbrath, 1983).

8) About 10% of the broad public in the U.S. report belonging to an environmental organization but a much smaller percentage (perhaps around 1%) are active (Mitchell, 1980a; Milbrath, 1981b). This active group tends to be well educated and middle class.

9) We have already indicated that the movement is opposed by defenders of the DSP but it is significant that no broad anti-environmental movement has been generated. Environmentalism is perceived as valuable by most people; therefore, those who might wish to oppose the movement do not feel they can openly be anti-environmental. Even Ronald Reagan and James Watt claim that they are environmentalists.

10) At the levels of the state and federal governments, there is a great deal of cooperation among environmental groups in supporting or opposing legislation and in transmitting messages to public bureaucracies. Although there is a similar willingness to cooperate at the local level, most of the local groups act independently. There is remarkably little competition for members among groups although there can be competition for recognition. Since there already is considerable diversity within the movement, there has been little

pressure toward splintering. Many people belong to several environmental organizations and this cross-cutting of memberships is likely to reduce any tendency toward splintering.

11) Most groups are supported primarily by membership dues; they also hold money raising events and receive a few grants from foundations and private individuals.

12) Direct action tactics, such as marches, demonstrations, and boycotts, are used by the environmental vanguard but not frequently. Most of the actions are peaceful and within channels. There seems to be no disposition whatsoever for the movement to become violently revolutionary; at least not so far.

13) The emotional component of the environmental movement is very important. It is based on values that are cherished dearly by most members.

14) The beliefs of the movement are slowly being articulated into an ideology, a new environmental paradigm. This emerging paradigm seems to be widely shared at the elite level but within the rank and file of the organizations there still is considerable belief diversity (Stallings, 1973; Utrup, 1979).

15) Because of belief similarities, the movement has important linkages to the anti-nuclear movement, the peace movement, the women's movement, and the consumer movement. Environmental beliefs and values also are similar to what Inglehart (1971, 1977, 1981, 1982) conceptualizes as "post-materialism" (Watts and Wandesforde-Smith, 1981). Inglehart theorizes that contemporary young adults, raised in an era of material affluence, have downplayed material values while elevating post-material values such as participation, self-realization, environmental protection, and quality of life.

Correlates of Environmentalism

Why is it that some people become environmentalists and others do not? Writers for the popular media and scholars often try to answer such questions by using demographic categories such as sex, age, and social class. Normally, these categories are instructive since they stand for certain types of background and learning experiences. In the cases of environmentalists and non-environmentalists, however, demographic categories explain very little of the difference; Van Liere and Dunlap (1980) review a number of studies to arrive at this conclusion. Belief and value variables explain much more of the difference (Milbrath, 1979, 1981a). However, since a great deal of the research in this area has used demographic categories, it still will be useful to begin our inquiry by looking at those factors.

Environmentalism has been measured in a variety of ways in these studies. Usually an expression of a belief in or support for environmental protection is a central aspect of the measure. The choice of measure may affect the strength of the observed relationship (Van Liere and Dunlap, 1981) but seldom the direction. The generalizations that follow hold across many specific studies using many specific measures. An environmentalism scale that I have found useful appears in Appendix D. See Weigel and Weigel (1978) for another example.

Demographic Indicators

First, let's look at age as a correlate of environmentalism. Many studies have shown that younger persons are more environmentally oriented than older persons (Dillman and Christenson, 1975; Jackson, 1980; Buttell and Flinn, 1977, 1978b; Buttel, 1979; Honnold, 1981; McTeer, 1978; Mitchell, 1978, 1980b; Milbrath, 1981b). Simple self-interest helps to explain some of this relationship; undertaking several years of effort to clean up the environment can hardly be as important to someone who expects to live only another eight or ten years as it is to a person who is looking forward to sixty or more years of continued life. Additionally, vigorous physical contact with the natural environment, such as hiking, is likely to be much more attractive to a young person than an older person. Furthermore, environmental topics are likely to have been part of the curriculum for persons passing through the schools in the past ten years whereas those topics were largely unknown to people who went to school forty or fifty years ago. While the relationship between age and environmentalism typically is statistically significant, the correlations usually are fairly low (in the .20–.30 range).

Studies using gender as a variable show that females typically are more environmentally-oriented than males (McStay and Dunlap, 1982; Jackson, 1980; Merchant, 1980; Honnold, 1981; Ray, 1975). It was mentioned earlier that environmentalists tend to have a stronger and more generalized sense of compassion than non-environmentalists. In modern society, females are socialized to be more compassionate than males. Women are expected to be more nurturing and protective while males are expected to be aggressive and competitive. This nurturing and protective posture of females shows up particularly strongly in their opposition to nuclear power (Nelkin, 1981; Passino and Lounsbury, 1976; Reed and Wilkes, 1980), in desires for strong regulation against polluters, and in vigorous actions to protect people against the dangers of toxic wastes. For example, most of the indigenous leaders among the homeowners mobilized by the toxic waste crisis at Love Canal in Niagara Falls, New York, were women (Levine, 1982; Shaw and Milbrath, 1983).

The relationship between environmentalism and social class is quite complex and difficult to summarize in a few sentences. We noted earlier that much of the membership, and particularly the leadership, of environmental organizations comes from the middle class or upper middle class. It is often charged in polemical anti-environmental essays that the environmental movement is an upper class movement. Tucker (1977, 1982a, 1982b) assumes that economic self-interest is the major basis on which people choose their postures toward environmentalism. Since the people in the upper middle class already have good jobs and a sufficient supply of goods, they selfishly now would like to slow down economic growth so that they can continue to enjoy pristine nature. Poorer people, however, need more material goods and desire continued economic growth much more highly than they desire environmental protection. Tucker implies that environmentalism is a selfish action by a privileged class seeking to suppress the aspirations of those not so privileged. Is this portrait accurate?

Empirical studies of the relationship between environmentalism and social class do not support the portrait. Socio-economic status (SES) is weakly related to expressions of environmental concern and of support for environmental protection; there is contradictory evidence as to the direction of the relationship (Cutler, 1981; Buttel and Flinn, 1974, 1978b; Tognacci, and others, 1972; Devall, 1970a; Jackson, 1980; Koenig, 1975). In unraveling this mystery, it is important to remember that, while environmental concern is strong at all ranks of socio-economic status, the people who are active in environmental organizations come mainly from the middle class (Mitchell, 1980a); nearly all organizations with a broad base are led by people from the middle class. The implication that working class people have little interest in beautiful nature or in being free from pollution simply is not borne out by the facts. We pointed out above that working class people have a strong desire for intimate interaction with nature and recent studies investigating concern for a clean environment show no difference by social class (Utrup, 1978; Milbrath, 1981b; Mitchell, 1980b).

One of the reasons why summary measures of SES do not show clearcut relationships to environmentalism is that the components of what is normally thought of as class measurement (education, income and occupation) do not exhibit the same direction of relationship to environmentalism. Many studies have shown a small but significant positive relationship between education and awareness of the environment and levels of environmental concern (Tognacci, and others, 1972; Simon, 1971, Watkins, 1974, 1975; Buttel and Flinn, 1977, 1978a, 1978b; Buttel, 1979; Devall, 1970a; Mitchell, 1980a; Weigel, 1977). Over the last two decades, entire national populations have learned about environmental problems. It is impossible for a person to become concerned about something of which he is not aware. Education and even I.Q. (Horvat and Voelker, 1976) are significant influences speeding up the process of becoming aware. Environmental knowledge is complex and integrative; education and interest in learning are essential to grasping its meaning.

Income is correlated with education but, as a social influence, it acts quite differently from education. Economic self-interest seems to mediate much of the relationship between income and environmentalism (Rathbun and Lindner, 1980). What little relationship there is seems to be curvilinear; persons who are the highest and lowest in income tend to be a little less environmentally oriented than people in the middle (Watkins, 1975; Buttel and Flinn, 1978b; Mitchell, 1978, 1980b). Persons of very high income tend to be employed in business and business people tend to hold economic values more highly than environmental values. Very poor people also strongly desire a better economic situation. Persons of middle income tend to be highly educated and more environmentally aware, as we just noted. In regression analyses, income tends to wash out as an explanatory variable for environmental concern.

We unravel the mystery a little further when we turn to an examination of occupation. Many studies have used occupational status as a measure but the findings have been very equivocal; that is because it is the wrong kind of occupational measure to apply. It is much more relevant to categorize people in terms of their sector of employment. Persons who are primarily engaged in the production and sale of material goods (Cotgrove, 1982, calls it the market sector) tend to be less environmentally oriented than persons who primarily provide services (the non-market sector) (Cotgrove, 1982; Cotgrove and Duff, 1980; Sewell, 1971; see also Tables 3.1, 3.2 and 3.3 in this book). Governmental regulations in many countries inhibit persons engaged in extraction and manufacturing from discharging their wastes into the environment. This a bothersome burden, in terms of both time and money, that is resented by many people in the production sector; they claim it inhibits their ability to make money. Persons in the service sector also bear some cost of environmental protection but these costs are more camouflaged while the benefits of a safe and clean environment are more visible and highly valued. Miles (1978) set forth an apt new law, "Where you stand depends on where you sit." There are clear value differences with respect to the environment between these groups; persons in the production sector tend to value material goods more highly whereas persons in the service sector tend to value a clean environment more highly (Milbrath, 1981b, 1981d; Cotgrove, 1982). The direction of causation is not clear; are there initial differences in values that lead young people to choose careers in either the production sector or the service sector (Duff and Cotgrove, 1982) or, once people are on the job, are these values strongly taught and reinforced in each of these sectors? It is probable that both kinds of influences are at work to produce this difference. Simple measures of class status cannot capture the richness of the relationships just discussed; that is why they do a poor job of explaining environmentalism.

Cotgrove (1982) is the most prominent proponent of using sector of employment to explain environmentalism.

Our own data point to some tentative conclusions on the class location of environmentalists. At the level of ideology, the majority reject the ideology of market capitalism. . . . Their second main difference is in their lack of commitment to material and economic goals compared with the traditional left. Unlike the trade union officials, environmentalists share the dominant paradigm view that material and non-material values are antagonistic. But they plump for non-material goals and values. . . . Our analysis suggests that environmentalism is an expression of the interests of those whose class position in the 'non-productive' sector locates them at the periphery of the institutions and processes of industrial capitalist societies. . . . It is a protest against alienation from the processes of decision making, and the depoliticization of issues through the usurpation of policy decisions by experts, operating within the dominant economic values. . . . Their attack is not simply rooted in their subordinate position. It is also a challenge to the goals and values of the dominant class, and the structures and institutions through which these are realized. Environmentalists' rejection of beliefs in the efficacy of the market, risk-taking and reward for achievement, and of the overriding goal of economic growth and of economic criteria is a challenge to the hegemonic ideology which legitimates the institutions and politics of industrial capitalism. . . . What we are suggesting then is that any understanding of the quite different values and beliefs of environmentalists and industrialists is to be found in part in their relations to the core economic institutions of society. Environmentalists are drawn predominantly from a specific fraction of the middle class whose interests and values diverge markedly from other groups in industrial societies. (pp. 95–96)

Most studies that have examined the relationship between race and environmentalism have shown that blacks are less environmentally oriented than whites (Hershey and Hill, 1977–78; Rathbun and Lindner, 1980). The major economic-political preoccupation of American blacks has been to improve their economic situation and to achieve equal rights. Both of these important values have still not been realized by many blacks; given that, they are unlikely to take on a new cause that many of them perceive to be of lower priority (Kreger, 1973). There is little evidence that blacks actively oppose environmentalism; many of them are concerned about pollution and toxics (Cutler, 1981; U.A.W., 1973; Mitchell, 1978). The April, 1983, *New York Times*/CBS poll showed blacks equally concerned as whites to maintain high environmentally protective standards. It seems more valid to say that many blacks are simply indifferent. It appears there are very few messages and very few reinforcements in the black culture to encourage participation in the environmental movement.

Using Beliefs and Values to Explain Environmentalism

Measures of beliefs and values are much more highly correlated with environmentalism than demographic measures. Most of the belief and value differences between environmentalists and non-environmentalists have already been set forth in Table 2.1. It should be re-emphasized that these beliefs and values cluster into structures that, quite literally, are ideologies. The better educated and more sophisticated a person is, the more tightly organized this ideological structure becomes.

Even though one can specify important belief and value differences between environmentalists and non-environmentalists, it still begs the question, "Why do some people become environmentalists while others do not? " While self-interest explanations frequently are proffered, it often is not clear what one's self-interest truly is. Is it in the best interest of a wealthy businessman to acquire even more wealth or would his quality of life be more significantly improved if he had a clean and beautiful environment in which to live and recreate? Is it in the best interest of a poor laborer to emphasize economic values and jobs while requiring him to breathe polluted air, fish and swim in polluted water, and be exposed to toxic poisons?

Early childhood experiences are probably quite important. Persons who learn early in life to love and cherish nature are likely to retain that value; it is likely to influence later decisions with respect to training and career choice. Similarly, persons who develop compassionate personalities learn how to empathize with and feel the suffering of other peoples, other species, and other generations. This naturally leads them to take a wider range of factors into consideration and to take a longer time perspective; such persons are much more likely to see the importance of environmental protection (Borden and Francis, 1978; Milbrath, 1975, 1979).

An explanatory factor that is not often considered, but which is vitally important for understanding environmentalism, is social learning. Society is slowly being forced to recognize how humans are injuring their environment. Most persons who have become environmentalists have gone through the experience called "consciousness raising." Foreign students at my university often tell me that they had never thought of undertaking environmental studies and had not even been aware of environmental problems before taking one of my courses.

Consciousness raising is a total societal function; it is a necessary ingredient in social learning (Arbuthnot and Lingg, 1975; Milbrath, 1975). We mentioned earlier that most people in the United States became aware of pollution problems in the 1960s but did not become aware of resource depletion and toxic waste problems until the late 1970s; social learning was taking place in both instances. In social learning, nature is our most powerful teacher. When we begin to hurt seriously or when our world no longer works the way it is supposed to, it becomes very important to learn about this new environmental condition with which we must come to terms. Our studies show numerous instances where people have learned to become environmentalists (Milbrath, 1975; Milbrath 1981b, 1981c, 1981d); interestingly, there are almost no instances of people learning to become non or anti-environmentalists.

Information in Chapters 2 and 3 show that a good deal of relearning already has taken place. Many people have abandoned basic tenets of the DSP. There is substantial sentiment in favor of the values of the environmentalists even though the great mass of people do not have a clear picture of the new society envisioned by the vanguard. As a matter of fact, that vision is still being worked through by the vanguard. That working through process, in itself, will be very interesting to follow as this social change drama continues to unfold.

FIVE

The Politics of Social Change

Even though environmentalists individually, and to a certain extent collectively, may recognize that in order to protect the environment and their civilization they need to turn a whole society around, it is highly unlikely that the vanguard would ever get together to decide on a strategy for bringing this about. People who are involved in stimulating and leading this social change (movement) are scattered in thousands of communities and engaged in millions of activities that contribute, each in its own small way, to the overall effort to influence social change. For the most part, they are not organized into political parties, they do not have a tightly organized and disciplined leadership cadre, they do not have a chosen articulate leader, they do not have a doctrine, and they do not even have a clearly identifiable enemy. Environmentalism is truly a grassroots movement with its own indigenous leaders in thousands of different settings. How can such a disparate group form a coalition strong enough to turn a whole society around? The question is rhetorical to illustrate the magnitude of the task; most environmentalists would not aspire so grandly.

Environmentalists tend to operate in at least three time frames simultaneously: first, many of them are urgently concerned about immediate problems such as toxics leaking from chemical waste dumps. The sense of immediate urgency that results from a local crisis recruits many new people to the movement. Second, they are concerned about medium range public policy such as appropriate legislation to protect the air and the water, to plan and control land use, to assure adequate resources, and so forth. Third, environmentalists try to educate people and stimulate a fundamental revolution in the way that people interpret how their world works and in how they live their lives. Public education, in school but also via the media and personal discussions, is a very large component of the environmental thrust for change.

Even though environmentalists have become very disenchanted with the unresponsiveness of government, their sense of urgency compels them to try to influence government because they perceive it to be a major lever for forestalling catastrophe and fostering social change. Like it or not, then, environmentalists who want to turn a society around must get involved in politics.

Perceived Need for Social Change

Do people recognize that there is a need for change in the social system? Are people ready for social change? What kind of change do

81

they foresee as necessary to solve environmental problems? Table 5.1 reports the exact wording of a question used in the 1980 study cross-tabulated against the rearguard-vanguard dimension that was developed and discussed in Chapter 3 (only U.S. data are reported here because a crucial question for the rearguard-vanguard dimension was not asked in England and Germany in 1980). The table discloses that hardly anybody believed there was no environmental problem and the few that did were mainly in the rearguard. A modest percentage believed that no basic change was needed to solve these problems and they also were mainly clustered in the rearguard or in the nature conservationist types. By far, the greatest percentage of people believed that a considerable amount of change is needed to solve environmental problems and these percentages are quite a bit higher toward the vanguard end of the index. Curiously, the modest percentages that believed a completely new system is needed, or that change is needed but it is unattainable, seem to be scattered across all of the types. When we cross-tabulated this question against the public and leadership groups in all three countries (see Table 7 in Appendix C) we also found a random scattering of the public and various elite groups choosing a completely new system or asserting that change is unattainable. These results suggest that certain people were not very serious in responding to this question and may have been using it as an occasion to give a gratuitous "boot" to the system.

Table 7 in Appendix C shows that only a small fraction of environmentalists thought no basic change was needed and most of them indicated that considerable change was needed; the percentage choosing a completely new system was not very different from that of other groups. Another clear pattern from that table is that the other elite groups were much more likely than the public to believe that no basic change was needed in our system in order to solve environmental

TABLE 5.1

"How much change do you think will be necessary in our social, economic and political system in order to solve our environmental problems?"

(Percentages of each type on the rearguard-vanguard dimension choosing each response.)

U.S. 1980	Rearguard 1	2	3	4	5	6	Vanguard 7	8
There is no environmental problem.	5	2	4	1	0	0	0	0
No basic change is needed to solve these problems.	44	20	20	11	35	16	9	5
A considerable amount of change is needed to solve these problems.	34	52	59	66	53	57	77	75
A completely new system is needed.	8	14	9	12	6	16	8	16
Change is needed but it is unattainable.	9	12	9	10	6	11	6	4

problems; this tendency was particularly strong for business leaders but also somewhat characteristic of public officials; however, even in these groups, a majority believed that considerable social change was required.

Urgency of Environmental Problems

The sense of urgency with which people in a country view their environmental problems is another important contextual factor in the politics of social change. The samples in the three-nation study rated the urgency of 10 different environmental problems on a seven-point scale that is shown along the vertical axis in Figure 5.1. The ten environmental problems were:

1) Noise
2) Air pollution
3) Water pollution
4) Over population
5) Solid waste disposal
6) Toxic wastes
7) Nuclear waste
8) Destruction of land and townscapes
9) Depletion of natural resources
10) Energy

Noise tended to have the lowest sense of urgency. Energy was highest in urgency in 1980 but declined somewhat by 1982 and, at that point, was rated at about the same level as the rest of the environmental problems. Although there were some interesting differences in perceived urgency across these problems, by different groups and different countries, it would take us too far afield to detail them here.

Factor analysis disclosed that people had a generalized level of urgency and concern; all of the urgency items were highly intercorrelated. These high correlations made it reasonable to calculate a mean urgency score for each respondent; these scores were aggregated for each group by country and are reported in Figure 5.1. As the reader can see, the perceived urgency levels for environmental problems were quite high, with nearly all of the means at 5 or above on a seven-point scale. As might be expected, environmentalists indicated higher urgency levels while business leaders and public officials felt a little less urgency. The Germans, in all groups, expressed higher levels of urgency than were found in the other countries. The public and labor leaders in England felt higher levels of urgency than did the public officials and business leaders. U.S. business leaders had the lowest sense of urgency. There was a slight decline in overall urgency from 1980 to 1982 in each group for each country; declines in England were a bit sharper than

Figure 5.1

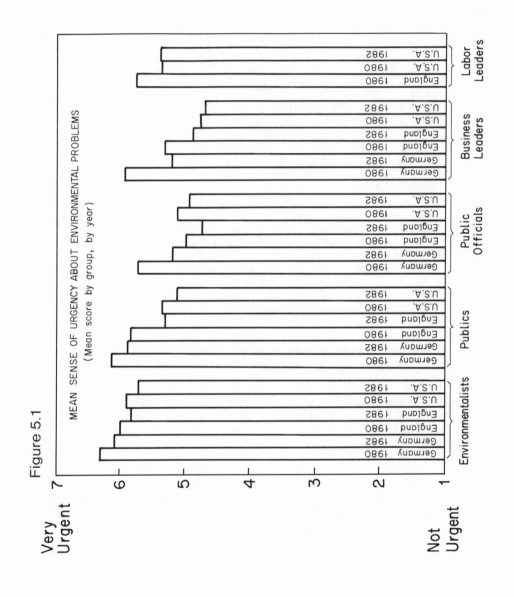

MEAN SENSE OF URGENCY ABOUT ENVIRONMENTAL PROBLEMS
(Mean score by group, by year)

in Germany or the United States. Even so, these urgency levels were still very high in 1982.

This generally high level of urgency about environmental problems did not translate very effectively into action; the measures of urgency showed only weak correlations with several measures of environmental behavior. It appears from the data that people are not quite sure what action might meaningfully alleviate their sense of urgency. Most of them do not look upon government as an effective actor for solving these problems; there was a clear tendency for people with a high sense of urgency to perceive governmental actions as inadequate; such persons also were more likely to trust environmental groups but distrust industry to help solve environmental problems. In addition, there was a weak but clearly significant tendency for those having a high sense of urgency to favor direct political action (such as marches and demonstrations) in order to influence governmental decisions (see Figure 5.3 on page 91 for item wording). Persons having a high sense of urgency also were likely to disbelieve that more and better technology could solve environmental problems; they believed instead that we will have to undergo considerable social change, including change in lifestyles, in order to deal with these problems. Interestingly, and also quite significantly, this sense of urgency had no relationship to traditional left-right political positions.

Perceived Adequacy of Governmental Actions

In each country, a preponderance of people perceived the government's actions as more inadequate than adequate on a seven-point scale shown along the vertical axis in Figure 5.2. This sense of inadequacy was particularly characteristic of environmentalists and the general public. Conversely, public officials (as one might expect) and business leaders were a little less disappointed in governmental actions; but even their judgements leaned more to the inadequate end of the scale. Curiously, in both the United States and England, business leaders saw governmental actions as a bit more satisfactory than did the public officials themselves.

Citizens' belief in the adequacy of their government for dealing with environmental problems was somewhat lower in England than in the U.S. and considerably lower than in Germany where the mean figures (with the exception of environmentalists) were fairly close to the middle of the scale. Our data show that the Germans are significantly more likely than the people in the other two countries to trust government and political parties to deal with environmental problems.

The raw data on which Figure 5.2 is based show that people's perceptions of the adequacy of government are distributed rather widely across the seven-point scale; why is it that some people perceive the government as inadequate while others do not? Demographic variables were of little help in answering this question. They did show that elected

Figure 5.2

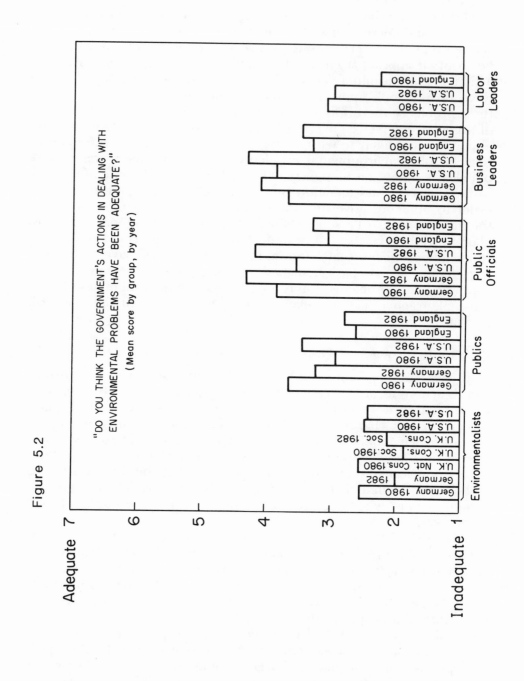

"DO YOU THINK THE GOVERNMENT'S ACTIONS IN DEALING WITH
ENVIRONMENTAL PROBLEMS HAVE BEEN ADEQUATE?"

(Mean score by group, by year)

public officials from small towns and rural areas were especially likely to perceive governmental actions as adequate; little else is worth reporting. There were stronger correlates among the belief and value items. The strongest correlate, not only among the public but across all of the elite groups (average r = .37), was a perception that humans are seriously damaging nature; the greater the perceived damage, the greater the perceived inadequacy of government. Business leaders, who were more likely than others to see governmental action as adequate, tended to deal with allegations of damage by denying that there was *serious* damage to nature. Position on the environmentalism scale (see Appendix D for wording) was highly positively correlated with a perception that government was dealing inadequately with environmental questions.

Environmentally-relevant Behavior

Citizens who feel that something should be done to solve environmental problems often have difficulty knowing how to act constructively to resolve those problems. It is even more difficult to know what might meaningfully be done if a person believes that resolution of the problems requires major social change. A third consideration is that it takes a great deal more effort and determination for a person to get out and do something than it does to simply think that something should be done. For all of these reasons, only a small proportion of the people who believe that something should be done actually get out and do something. This gap between belief and behavior is applicable to political behavior in general, not simply to environmentally-relevant behavior (Milbrath and Goel, 1982, pp. 49–51).

Some environmentally-relevant activities can be undertaken by individuals acting alone; we typically find higher percentages of people doing these things than engaging in activities that must be done in coordination with others in order to be successful. In our 1980 study, we inquired if respondents engaged in six possible behaviors relevant to environmental problems; they are listed in Table 8 of Appendix C along with a report of the percentage for each group in each country that engaged in the behavior with some regularity. Three of the behaviors can be undertaken by individuals without coordination with others; they are:

1) Regularly separating household rubbish for recycling.
2) Taking into account the amount of packaging on goods when shopping.
3) Being inclined to complain to someone in authority in case the individual observes a bad case of pollution.

Three other behaviors generally are taken in concert with others:
1) Participating actively on environmental issues.

2) Belonging to environmental groups.
3) Belonging to nature conservation associations.

Overall, we find more of the public participating individually than in concert with others in all three countries. Germans were much more likely to act individually than to participate through groups. The Americans, in contrast, were not as likely as Germans to take individual action such as recycling or considering packaging on goods, but were more likely than the Germans to join and participate in groups. Percentages in England fell somewhere between these two extremes. These findings support other scattered bits of evidence in the study that Germans have a weaker tradition for group political activity than the English or the Americans. This may affect their conduct of politics. We shall see later in the chapter that Germans were somewhat more likely than Americans or English to favor unconventional direct action in politics.

Although the general public, in all countries, is more likely to take individual than collective behavior, it is not so characteristic of the elites who are much more accustomed to group activity. Interestingly, elites (with the exception of environmental leaders) in each country were more likely to join conservation groups than to join environmental groups. Most elites, being part of the establishment, are not likely to join groups advocating their displacement. In the United States, where the distinction between environmental and conservation groups is not so clear as in Germany and England, this pattern did not hold for public officials or labor leaders.

Are Present Political Structures Appropriate for Environmental Action?

Left-Right Ideology and Environmentalism

The reader will recall from the two-dimensional display in Figure 2.1 that the left-right argument is between socialists and capitalists but has little relevance for environmental problems. Even though the left-right division presumably is relevant for political party contesting in the U.S., it is not perceived as especially relevant by many voters. The left-right argument is fading from relevance in Germany and England as well. As we have tried to show in this book, the conflict between the rearguard and the environmental vanguard is much more fundamental to the nature of society in each of these countries and may become relevant in the future for political contesting between political parties. Despite this, the left-right frame of reference for thinking about politics continues to dominate political discourse.

Quite a number of scholars have investigated the relationship between beliefs on the left-right continuum and environmental beliefs and values (Constantini and Hanf, 1972; Dillman and Christenson, 1972; Buttel and Flinn, 1976; Van Liere and Dunlap, 1980; Weigel, 1977; Springer and Constantini, 1974; Buttel and Johnson, 1977). Generally, these studies have shown that there is a modest tendency for persons who are oriented toward environmental protection to be left-leaning as compared to those less concerned about the environment. Our study supports this generalization; Table 9 in Appendix C reports the percentages of each sample in the three countries that assign themselves to a position on a five-position left-right scale. In each country, environmentalists are slightly more left-leaning than the general public. Note also that in England, the conservation society members (vanguard) clearly lean left while the nature conservationists lean right. It also can be seen in that table that there is a sharp difference between labor leaders who traditionally lean left and business leaders who traditionally lean right.

Even though environmentalists are left-leaning, the table also shows that environmentalists are more likely than other elites to say they have no position on this dimension; this is especially true in Germany where the motto of the Green Party is, "We are neither left nor right; we are in front" (Capra and Spretnak, 1984). This tendency was confirmed in another U.S. study (see Continental Group Report, 1982). Substantial proportions of the public also indicate that they have no position.

Essentially the left-right dimension reflects the contrast between those preferring a laissez faire society to those preferring a more managed society. We generally found that beliefs on this dimension were more strongly correlated with beliefs related to market mechanisms, public ownership of property, maintaining differential reward structures, and cooperation vs. competition than we found them to correlate with environmental beliefs. This means that, in each of the countries, environmentalists seeking socio-political reform confront a party structure that is oriented toward arguments about the economic management of society; it is a structure that does not readily reflect environmental concerns except as they can be translated into an economic management framework.

Readiness to Change Parties

Would people make use of a party structure that more adequately reflected environmental concerns? Do people feel sufficiently strongly about environmental matters that they would be willing to change their party, or their traditional vote, if that action presented an opportunity to serve environmental values? In 1982, respondents in all three countries were asked, "Would you be influenced in your choice of party at the next election by its policy on environmental questions? " (this question was also asked in 1980 in England and the U.S.). Table 10 in Appendix C shows that about 20% of the public in each of the three countries indicated that they probably would change their vote under those circumstances; another sizable percentage reported that they possibly would do so. The reader will recall from Chapter 3 that persons in the vanguard were more ready to change than were persons in the rearguard. Environmentalists, particularly in the United States, indicated a high probability of doing so. Business leaders especially, but also labor leaders and public officials in England, were much more likely to indicate they would *not* do so. Party attachment of leaders in England seem to be considerably stronger than in the U.S.

Readiness to Use Direct (Unconventional) Political Action

If political structures are not appropriate, or if people perceive that governmental officials are not listening or responding to their pleas, citizens may turn to extraordinary means to try to achieve their objectives. In this study, we refer to this phenomenon as "direct action." Frequent news stories from many countries tell of environmentalists taking direct action in the form of marches, protests, sit-ins, etc. We asked respondents the question that is shown at the top of Figure 5.3 which was responded to according to the scale on the left margin. Responses were quite widely spread on this item but it clearly shows in the figure that more people oppose than support direct action, with the exception of environmentalists. This exceptional emphasis on direct action by environmentalists was particularly true in Germany but the general tendency also can be seen in the United States and England. This item showed a sharp contrast between the members of the Conservation Society and the members of the Somerset Trust for Nature Conservation in England; the latter group expressed even less support for direct action than did the general public in England. Public officials (with the exception of Germany in 1980) and business leaders were quite strongly opposed to unconventional direct action. People in the United States generally were opposed to direct action; business leaders were almost unanimously opposed.

What lies behind a readiness to take direct action? The strongest predictor in our study of a propensity to support direct action was a perception that man's activities were *severely* damaging nature; this generalization holds not only for the public but for elite groups as well (average $r = .47$). For the public, love of nature also led many people to support direct action. Among the elites, social policy concerns were mixed with love of nature as a total thrust toward direct action. The evidence is pretty clear that people turn to direct action because they strongly value things or they fervently believe in the policies they propose and are determined to do whatever they can to bring them into effect. Environmentalists probably will continue to use direct action to influence policy as long as they believe that they are unable to affect change through normal political channels.

We asked if people perceived that they had much influence on environmental questions as well as on local and national political decisions. In all three countries, most people believed that they had very little influence; this was even true of the elites although it also was

Figure 5.3

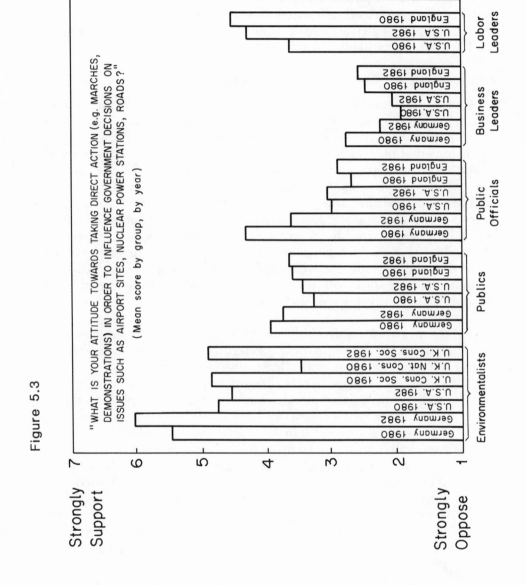

"WHAT IS YOUR ATTITUDE TOWARDS TAKING DIRECT ACTION (e.g. MARCHES, DEMONSTRATIONS) IN ORDER TO INFLUENCE GOVERNMENT DECISIONS ON ISSUES SUCH AS AIRPORT SITES, NUCLEAR POWER STATIONS, ROADS?"

(Mean score by group, by year)

Strongly
Support

Strongly
Oppose

clear that elites perceived they had more influence than did the general public. Generally, better educated persons from the upper classes, and males, were more likely to believe they could influence environmental policy. Many previous studies of political behavior have shown these same patterns (Milbrath and Goel, 1982 pp. 57–64). The strongest correlate of perceived influence was a higher rate of activity on an "environmental behavior index" (see Appendix D). Those who get out and act are more likely to feel that they have influence.

Trust in Groups to Solve Environmental Problems

A profound question for governance in all societies is the extent to which groups trust each other to make wise policy choices. In our study, we inquired about the trust that people had in various groups for solving environmental problems; each respondent rated each group on a seven-point "no trust—great trust" scale. Mean levels of trust were calculated for each group, by each group, for each country from the 1980 data and are reported in Table 11 in Appendix C. The 1982 data on trust were very similar and are not reported in order to avoid overcrowding an already jammed table. A great deal of information is presented in that table as a basic record of the study; certain means have been starred to help guide the reader in making comparisons. All of the possible comparisons will not be detailed here. Study of the table produced the following generalizations:

1) Each group tended to trust itself more than other groups trusted it. As might be expected, business leaders trusted environmental groups the least and vice versa.
2) Generally, highest levels of trust were accorded to scientists and technologists but environmentalists ran a close second. The public in Germany and England, however, trusted environmentalists more than scientists and technologists.
3) Generally, trust in scientists and technologists was negatively correlated with variables measuring environmentalism. This means that people with strong environmentally-oriented beliefs and values were more likely to have doubts about the benefits of science and technology; these benefits are accepted almost without question in other sectors of the society. Higher class persons with higher income were more likely to trust scientists and technologists.
4) Environmentalists were generally trusted in all sectors of society. Young people trusted them more than did older people. In the United States, females more likely trusted them than did males. Interestingly, persons of high education were slightly more likely to trust environmental groups whereas persons of high income were less likely to trust those groups.

5) Generally, Germans had a higher level of trust for all groups than that shown in other nations; this was particularly true of their trust in government. The English, in contrast, seemed to be less trusting in general, particularly of industry and scientists.

6) In all nations, industry, government and unions were not very highly trusted, with the unions trusted the least. Distrust of industry was negatively correlated with strong values for environmental protection. Just as young people were more likely to trust environmental groups, older people were more likely to trust industry.

7) Trust in government generally was quite low; this relates to the point made earlier that governmental actions on the environment are perceived as being inadequate. Public officials and business leaders assigned higher levels of trust to government than did environmentalists. In contrast to judgements about industry, however, trust in government was positively correlated with many of the indices measuring environmental concern. Curiously, persons having doubts about the value of science and technology were more likely to distrust government; that probably reflects a perception that government is a major promoter of science and technology.

8) Most groups in the U.S. had exceedingly low levels of trust in political parties for solving environmental problems. The level of trust in parties was a bit higher in England and still higher in Germany.

9) By and large, the same patterns of trust and distrust appear in each of these countries; they seem to have the same kind of internal political struggle.

10 Comparing the 1980 and 1982 data on trust showed there was a very slight decline in trust of all groups, in all three countries over the two-year period. Trust in science and technology declined more than that shown for other groups. Also the German public and business leaders showed a clear decline in trust of government.

11) In 1982, we asked separately about levels of trust people held in "environmental action groups" and "nature conservation associations." Nearly every group, in all three countries, trusted nature conservation associations slightly more than they trusted environmental action groups. It probably is easier to trust groups that are not striving to change the basic structure of the system. The direct action tactics often employed by environmental action groups leave many people feeling uneasy and distrustful; this is even true of many environmentalists.

Speculation on the Near-term Impact of Environmentalism on Societal Guidance

It is clear from the evidence presented in this chapter that environmentalists who are struggling for basic social change find very little responsiveness in present political and governmental structures. Environmentalists have had some impact in producing reform legislation and in reforming business practices with respect to preventing pollution. However, these "within system" actions do not constitute fundamental social change which must be seen in a longer time frame and can only come about as beliefs and values gradually change. This transformation may have comparatively little relationship to what is going on in the political arena. Yankelovich (1981, p. 36) paraphrases Daniel Bell to observe "that our culture has a dynamic thrust of its own, following a different 'axial principle' from that which regulates the economy or politics. We cannot deduce what is happening in the culture from events taking place in a political and economic arena."

The old DSP, with its left-right political contesting structure and its domination by the rearguard, can continue to exclude the environmental vanguard from having much affect on policy for quite some time into the future. The beliefs, practices, and achievements of the old DSP are attractive enough to a sufficient number of people that, if the contest were to be determined by attractiveness alone, they could continue to suppress the vanguard. Our data have shown that social learning has progressed apace and that many people have departed from some of the central beliefs of the DSP; but people will not be ready to give societal leadership to the vanguard so long as that DSP continues to perform reasonably adequately. If it turns out that the DSP is not sustainable, as the environmentalists argue, physical and societal events will force people to continue the relearning process. Should that happen, a substantial majority of the population will reject the DSP as unworkable, the political system and governments will then be more open to the efforts of the environmental vanguard to seize leadership. If our social relearning comes about in this way, as I suspect that it must, it will be very painful and disruptive but, as history reveals, this usually is the way that major social change comes about.

SIX

Can Modern-day Prophets Redirect Society?

Social change is always taking place, of course. Our physical world is constantly undergoing some kind of change (desertification, for example); our science and technology is constantly in evolution, and the relationships between humans are in constant flux. The question raised by this book (that may have to remain unanswered), is whether or not a group of humans can redirect the course of their civilization? The vanguard wishes to develop a civilization that can survive in a long-run sustainable relationship with the physical environment in which it is embedded as well as maximize quality of life for the people living in it. Social change seems to come about as a function of one or more of three processes: evolutionary succession, social learning, and scientific/technological development.

Evolutionary succession is a form of social change analogous to the evolution of species described by Darwin. There have been many societies in human history that made fundamental mistakes and faded away; the people living in them were conquered and carried away, or they abandoned the site, or simply died. Other societies, that have been more adaptive and made wiser decisions, have managed to survive; typically, they also expanded. Trial and error is the basic element in this kind of social change; it constitutes a type of social learning.[1] We cannot know whether our present civilization can adapt and make sufficiently wise decisions to be able to survive. Evolutionary learning can be very traumatic and painful for the people living in a society that crumbles because it cannot adapt to the physical realities of the environment in which it is embedded. The failure of one or a few small societies does not necessarily threaten the survival of the species. However, our present world faces an even greater danger because humans have acquired sufficient destructive power, that could be unleashed by a single tragic mistake, to destroy the biosphere support that humans require.

Social learning, such as that advocated by environmental modern-day prophets, is intended to be gradual and to take effect sooner so as to avoid social system collapse. How could this come about? The social learning process begins with a growing awareness that the present system is not working well. This is perceived first by an emerging elite who gather more adequate information and undertake analysis of society's ills. This growing awareness and new information eventually leads the elite to perceive a better way. Next, all of these (awareness, information, new ideas) have to be communicated to other members of society. As more and more people are enlightened, they may be persuaded to join

95

the movement. Sooner or later it will become obvious that the persons in the movement must try to affect governmental policies and, if possible, win elections. If they can be successful in this effort, the policies and messages coming from the government, and contained in the political discourse that always surrounds government, may further advance the desired social change.

It is possible, but very difficult, to bring about such a massive re-learning effort. If the systemic flaws pointed out by the modern-day prophets are in fact true, this suggests that the time for social learning is very short, that the chances of successful redirection before the old system breaks down are very slim. There may be a greater readiness to abandon old ideas and to accept new ones at the time of the breakdown but it could very well be too late to salvage many good things about present society. Redirecting society before the breakdown occurs is the enormous challenge that the modern-day prophets are urging us to meet.

Scientific/technological development has often been an especially powerful stimulus to social change. The steam engine, the automobile, nuclear power, and computers are obvious recent examples. Changes in the physical environment also can have that effect. As climates have changed, civilizations have died; others have sprung up in places that formerly could not support human life. Some scientists and environmentalists are now warning that the increased burning of fossil fuels will likely elevate the carbon dioxide content of the air sufficiently to create a "greenhouse effect" and raise the overall temperature of the earth by a few degrees. This will probably produce sufficient change in climate to force massive change in agriculture. It also could result in the gradual melting of the polar icecaps, which would raise the level of the oceans by as much as 30 feet, flooding a substantial portion of human settlements. Such a human-induced physical change surely would result in major social change. Social change caused by technological development, or by significant change in the physical environment, is difficult to foresee and nearly impossible to plan on.

Some people have dismissed the warnings of environmentalists on the ground that technological breakthroughs are likely to occur that will save us from our looming environmental predicament. For example, scientists have worked for many years trying to control and harness fusion power (the same power as in the hydrogen bomb). If they could succeed, it would help relieve the energy shortage we will experience as fossil fuels are depleted. Our recent history of technological devel-opment has been sufficiently impressive that we should continue search-ing for technological solutions. But, environmentalists ask, how certain is it that a technological solution will be sufficient to save us? Should we rely on a technical breakthrough and not take the fork in the road to a different society? Is our present way of life so attractive and the promise of technological deliverance so certain that we can complacently continue on our present course?

Where Are We Now?

Would we recognize a fundamental change if we were living in the midst of it? It is difficult to tell how fundamental it is until we have lived through it. The changes already underway that we have tried to document in this book, could conceivably be halted. History may disclose that this particular struggle for "a better way" may be only a "blip" in the long run thread of history. Environmentalists may come to be seen as heretics rather than as prophets. On the other hand, it also is conceivable that we are in the midst of a social change that is as fundamental, deep and lasting as the industrial revolution which laid the basis for our present societies.

Let's review the evidence to estimate where we are now. For more than twenty years, the modern-day prophets have been warning their fellow humans to mend their ways or suffer dire consequences. As a prime example, Rachel Carson, in her book *The Silent Spring* published in 1962, warned us of far-reaching, ecological damage from pesticides. A sufficient number of these prophesies/calamities have come true that environmentalists have gained a good deal of credibility. Pollution problems have become so ubiquitous that more than 100 national governments have set up environmental protection agencies. Some of today's worst pollution problems are in "third world" countries, especially those trying to industrialize. Human population has increased so rapidly in many countries that coping with the crush has taken on an air of crisis. Minerals have become sufficiently scarce, especially fossil energy, to disrupt many economies and to subject all of them to high inflation. The pressures of human population and human exuberance are destroying farmland and forests, creating deserts, and driving many species into extinction.

Many people in the U.S. (20% to 30%) believe that we have made good progress in dealing with our environmental problems but even more (40% to 50%) believe that we are losing ground. The overall consensus in the three countries we have examined is that our societal response to environmental problems has been inadequate. Most people, in most countries, if they are aware of environmental problems at all, have little sense that anything effective is being done. Overall, it is fair to say at this point that, most people in advanced industrial societies are aware of environmental problems, that awareness is growing, and environmental concerns have assumed a permanent place on the public agenda. They also are emerging on the agenda in most developing countries.

Social change begins, and is most fundamentally and widely expressed, in the beliefs and values of the people. Data from these three advanced industrial countries clearly show that there is widespread awareness of environmental problems, that they are perceived as a large set of problems, that people are highly concerned and are willing to support fairly drastic action to meet those problems.

The reader is invited to review Table 2.1 (p. 22) that lists and contrasts the beliefs and values of the dominant social paradigm that is defended by the rearguard and a new environmental paradigm advocated by the vanguard. Our data disclose that a vanguard has been formed and is preparing itself to meaningfully contest socially and politically with the rearguard as it tries to redirect modern society. We also can see that the mass of people have more readily abandoned DSP beliefs than most elites who have a greater stake in, and commitment to, the present system. Despite this important social fact, substantial numbers of the elites also have abandoned DSP beliefs and some have even joined the vanguard. We may anticipate that this battle for people's minds will continue for some time into the future.

As indicated in Figure 2.1, the mass of people are located somewhere between the rearguard and the vanguard. They love and value nature but they also want to use nature to produce goods. They see humans interrelated with nature and wish to avoid blind domination of nature, but also have widely adopted technology to exploit nature. They desire economic growth but they desire environmental protection even more; they believe that their society can protect the environment and still manage to grow in certain qualitative ways (see also Continental Group Report, 1982). Even Jack Kemp, a strong defender of the DSP, recognizes the subtle difference:

> Inflated growth means *quantity* growth. Real growth, the kind that must be promoted if democratic capitalism is to survive, is *quality* growth. The difference is crucial. Quantity can only grow at the expense of the planet. Quality is a boundless concept. (1979, p. 7)

The public is fairly aware that certain technological developments, production processes, and waste disposal practices have the potential to inflict injury on innocent people. They support regulations and procedures to insure that these activities do not place people at undue risk. Most people have begun to recognize that there are resource shortages, that limits must be placed on population growth, that we must learn to conserve rather than blindly rush to produce and consume, and that there are limits to growth. The idea of limits to growth is almost universally accepted in Germany, is widely accepted in England, but continues to be highly disputed in the United States.

Even though people in these advanced industrial societies continue to accept capitalism and the DSP, they do desire substantial modification of many of its basic tenets. Our data show that they sense that they have given away too much of the control of their lives to a political-economic system that emphasizes high-powered production, maximizing wealth, decisions by experts, etc.; they want an open society with many opportunities for citizen participation even if it should slow things down. They have begun to recognize that the market cannot provide most public goods and that taxes and regulation must be used to insure their provision. Competition is being tempered by an equal or greater emphasis on cooperation. The negative aspects of complex and fast lifestyles are being discovered, leading many people to turn to simpler lifestyles that are rich in a different way. All in all, material economic values are being displaced by a wider range of quality of life values.

Where are we Likely to be Going?

It was difficult enough to estimate where we are at the present time; it is even more difficult to estimate where we are going. In making such estimates, there is a natural desire to be optimistic. People need to have a belief that things can get better—that reform is possible. Readers don't like to be told that reform is hopeless, that nothing can be done to improve the situation. Of course reform is possible, but is it probable? What can we realistically expect to happen?

From the perspective of the modern-day prophets who foresee the need for and desire social change, there is comfort in the fact that we have already come so far. Even though it seems dreadfully slow, social learning is really taking place. There already is significant departure from the old DSP. Many of the values and beliefs of the NEP have already been substantially accepted. For example, the attempt by the Reagan administration in the U.S. to diminish the national emphasis on environmental protection is being successfully rebuffed.

But, can this momentum be continued? The rearguard has recognized the challenge of the vanguard and has regrouped its forces for a vigorous defense. The rearguard recently won control of the national governments in all three of these advanced industrial societies. The vanguard is clearly not strong enough at present to successfully contend with the rearguard. The material values and the material achievements of the old DSP continue to have their allure and a flood of modern advertising bends every effort to maintain that allure. If the choice between the NEP and the DSP was merely a matter of individual preference, the DSP would win. We would go on producing, consuming, and discarding with the same abandon as before.

But do we have the option to keep it all going? Is there a sufficient resource base to support it? Can our biosphere tolerate the wastes that we produce and discard? Can we accept the risks and vulnerabilities of intricate technologies and management systems that do not readily tolerate human failure? In sum, have we built a civilization that we can sustain? The rearguard says, yes, and the vanguard says, no.

It is often said among environmentalists, who are frustrated or disappointed that people are so slow to respond to their warnings, that people are not really going to learn until we get into a crisis. Then people will cast off the shackles of their old beliefs, their minds will be open, and they will be able to receive and act upon the vision of the NEP vanguard. Most of the people in the vanguard hold the belief that the prospects for constructive social change are pessimistic in the near and medium term future, but are mildly optimistic in the long run. This optimism is based not so much on the innate attractiveness of the new paradigm they propose but rather on the pressure toward relearning that they believe will be forced upon us by nature itself as our resources begin to run out, our biosphere increasingly is poisoned, and our old socio-economic-political systems begin to collapse. Some believe that efforts to reform, at the point of collapse, will be too late. Others believe that it already is too late. But, most environmentalists keep trying to bring about change in the hope that society can be redirected in time to avoid a catastrophe.

Of course, the rearguard defenders scoff at these ideas. They believe that our environmental problems are not really serious and can be solved by technological development, that human ingenuity can solve our resource problems, that an expanding and exuberant society can tolerate and survive risks, that material wealth should be the central objective of society, and that our socio-economic-political system is fundamentally sound. If they are correct in these assumptions, there can be little doubt that the dominant social paradigm will continue to be dominant. However, the central question posed by the environmentalists returns, can it be sustained?

Assume for a moment that the environmentalists are right and that the system cannot be sustained, that we will experience crisis after crisis as well as serious system breakdown. Can we then, realistically, expect that we will quickly relearn and take corrective actions to extricate ourselves from our predicament? Can we expect that people will be foresighted, optimistic, creative, and cooperative as we struggle to find our way in a crisis situation? Actually, there is good reason to expect that many people, probably the majority, will simply give up when their world begins to disintegrate; for many it will be easier to die than to struggle. Realistically, we must recognize that it is probable that our civilization will fail, forcing the human race, once more, into learning by evolutionary succession.

Personally, as I contemplate these possibilities, I find it unacceptable to adopt the posture of the rearguard; if they are wrong, we are lost. There is sufficient credibility to the warnings of the modern-day prophets that we must take them seriously. If the prophets can convince us to follow their lead onto a new path, we have a chance to save the best in our civilization and a chance for a reasonable quality of life for most people. If they are wrong, there is not likely to be a catastrophe and all we will have lost is the chance to have lived our lives with greater gusto and exuberance. It is often charged by the defenders of the rearguard that environmentalists want to take us back to the caves. This is a simplistic argument used by defenders of the DSP to avoid the challenge to develop a new and better society. The vanguard does not renounce all technology, all industrial production, all growth, or all material goods. Environmentalists advocate thoughtful consideration of where we are going, careful and subdued production and consumption, conservation of resources, protection of the environment, and the basic values of love, compassion, justice, and quality of life.

In modern society, we have developed a socio-technical-economic system that can dominate and destroy nature. Alongside it, we have retained a normative and ethical system based on 2000-year-old religions. The lack of congruence between these two systems threatens the continued existence of our civilization. Our science tells us how our world works physically but provides no moral guidance for our behavior within it. The normative prescriptions from inherited religions do not address the power and exuberance of modern human activities. The environmental modern-day prophets are trying to unite a sophisticated understanding of how the world works with a new normative/ethical system that recognizes and addresses those realities. Only time will tell whether they will be listened to as they try to lead society in a new direction.

NOTES

1. Two prominent social scientists who place great emphasis on evolutionary learning as the major way that societies advance are Kenneth Boulding, *Ecodynamics: A New Theory of Societal Evolution,* Beverly Hills: Sage 1978; and Raoul Naroll, *The Moral Order: An Introduction to the Human Situation,* Beverly Hills: Sage 1983.

INTERNATIONAL ENVIRONMENT SURVEY

(How to Fill Out This Questionnaire)   ☐ ☐ ☐ ☐

This questionnaire primarily seeks your opinion. There are <u>no right or wrong answers</u>. It will be apparent that many questions deal with the environment. Please don't tell us what you think we want to hear. These are complicated problems with conflicting values. ' Please tell us <u>what you really think</u>.

As you know, the same word can mean different things to different people; hence, it is impossible to find a general wording to exactly suit every person. Please bear with us if the wording of an item doesn't seem quite right to you from time to time and do your best to answer the question. We hope we have gotten the wording "right" for you most of the time.

Please pay close attention to the directions for each part of the questionnaire. Generally, you will indicate your response by circling a number on a scale.

For example, some questions ask you to choose between opposing views:

I prefer warm weather ☐3 ⊛2 ☐1 ☐0 ☐1 ☐2 ☐3 I prefer cold weather

If you strongly prefer one or the other you would circle a ☐3. If you have no preference, can't decide, or don't know, you would circle a ☐0. If you have a slight preference you would circle a ☐1 or a ☐2 depending on the strength of your preference. Other items will use other kinds of scales which are self-evident. In each case <u>circle one response</u>.

<u>Many thanks for your help!</u>

Here are a number of statements about society and the environment. <u>Please circle the number</u> that comes closest to expressing the extent of your agreement or disagreement with the item.

		strongly disagree						strongly agree
C 1.1	There are likely to be serious and disruptive shortages of essential raw materials if things go on as they are.	-3	-2	-1	0	1+	2+	3+
C 1.2	The storage of nuclear wastes is too dangerous.	-3	-2	-1	0	1+	2+	3+
C 1.3	Industrial societies provide a high level of well-being for most people who live in them.	-3	-2	-1	0	1+	2+	3+
C 1.4	We are approaching the limit of the number of people the earth can support.	-3	-2	-1	0	1+	2+	3+
C 1.5	A nuclear accident resulting in the contamination of the environment is increasingly likely.	-3	-2	-1	0	1+	2+	3+
C 1.6	The good effects of technology outweigh its bad effects.	-3	-2	-1	0	1+	2+	3+
C 1.7	We are fast using up the world's oil resources.	-3	-2	-1	0	1+	2+	3+
C 1.8	Humans must live in harmony with nature in order to survive.	-3	-2	-1	0	1+	2+	3+
C 1.9	There is a need for nuclear power.	-3	-2	-1	0	1+	2+	3+

			strongly disagree						strongly agree

C 1.10 Science and technology are our best hope for the future.   -3   -2   -1   0   1+   2+   3+

C 1.11 Economically disruptive energy shortages are likely to become more frequent if we go on as we are.   -3   -2   -1   0   1+   2+   3+

C 1.12 There are limits to growth beyond which our industrialized society cannot expand.   -3   -2   -1   0   1+   2+   3+

1.13 We are being involved less and less in important decisions which shape our lives.   -3   -2   -1   0   1+   2+   3+

1.14 We are in danger of letting technology run away with us.   -3   -2   -1   0   1+   2+   3+

1.15 Pollution is rising to dangerous levels.   -3   -2   -1   0   1+   2+   3+

1.16 The balance of nature is very delicate and easily upset.   -3   -2   -1   0   1+   2+   3+

1.17 Mankind is severely abusing the environment.   -3   -2   -1   0   1+   2+   3+

The following are contrasting statements about emphases or directions our society should be taking. Please circle a numbered box on the scale indicating the extent of preference you have for one or the other emphasis for our society.

C 2.1 A society that emphasizes economic growth.   [3] [2] [1] [0] [1] [2] [3]   A society that limits economic growth.

C 2.2 A society that emphasizes being careful not to harm nature.   [3] [2] [1] [0] [1] [2] [3]   A society that emphasizes using nature to produce more consumer goods.

C 2.3 A society which attaches relatively less importance to law and order.   [3] [2] [1] [0] [1] [2] [3]   A society which attaches relatively more importance to law and order.

C 2.4 A society that plans to avoid risks in the production of wealth.   [3] [2] [1] [0] [1] [2] [3]   A society that recognizes that risks are unavoidable in the production of wealth.

C 2.5 A society that emphasizes economic rewards for initiative and achievement.   [3] [2] [1] [0] [1] [2] [3]   A society that ensures a minimum standard of living for everyone.

C 2.6 A society which emphasizes work which is humanly satisfying.   [3] [2] [1] [0] [1] [2] [3]   A society where work is controlled mainly by economic needs.

C 2.7 A society that emphasizes foresight and planning for the public good.   [3] [2] [1] [0] [1] [2] [3]   A society that relies on the supply and demand market to maximize the public good.

C 2.8 A society with many chances for citizens to have a say in government and which expects its citizens to give some time to politics.   [3] [2] [1] [0] [1] [2] [3]   A society with few chances for citizens to have a say in government and which doesn't expect its citizens to give much time to politics

C 2.9 A society which recognizes differences in income related to skill, education and achievement.   [3] [2] [1] [0] [1] [2] [3]   A society which emphasizes similar incomes for everyone.

C2.10 A society in which people are judged by the kinds of people they are. ③ ② ① ⓪ ① ② ③ A society in which people are judged largely by what they have achieved.

C2.11 A society in which there is an emphasis on rules which are the same for everybody. ③ ② ① ⓪ ① ② ③ A society in which personal considerations play a large part.

C2.12 A society that emphasizes environmental protection over economic growth. ③ ② ① ⓪ ① ② ③ A society that emphasizes economic growth over environmental protection.

Please circle the response that best expresses your view.

In selecting a location for a vacation, how important are the following?

	not at all important					very important	
C 3.1 A clean and attractive landscape	1	2	3	4	5	6	7
C 3.2 The opportunity to make contact with others easily	1	2	3	4	5	6	7
C 3.3 Isolated and unspoiled nature	1	2	3	4	5	6	7
C 3.4 Interesting sights (museums, monuments)	1	2	3	4	5	6	7
C 3.5 Exotic cultures	1	2	3	4	5	6	7
C 3.6 Adventure	1	2	3	4	5	6	7
C 3.7 Good shopping	1	2	3	4	5	6	7
C 3.8 Cheap food and accommodation	1	2	3	4	5	6	7

C 3.9 Do you separate your household rubbish (e.g. glass, paper) for recycling?

```
         never                        always
          1    2    3    4    5    6    7
```

C3.10 Is it easy or difficult for you to find a recycling station?

```
         difficult                     easy
          -1   -2   -3    0   1+   2+   3+
```

C3.11 Do you take into account the amount of packaging on goods when you buy?

```
         never                        always
          1    2    3    4    5    6    7
```

C3.12 Do you participate actively on environmental issues?

    a) no
    b) yes

C3.13 Do you belong to any environmental groups?

    a) no
    b) yes, one or two
    c) yes, three or more

C3.14 Do you belong to any nature conservation association?

    a) no
    b) yes, one or two
    c) yes, three or more

C3.15 If you observed a bad case of pollution, would you know where to take a complaint?

    a) no
    b) not sure
    c) yes, definitely

C3.16 How likely would you be to complain to someone in authority?

    a) not likely
    b) somewhat likely
    c) very likely

3.17 Have you ever complained to someone in authority?

      a) no
      b) yes

How urgent are the following environmental problems in this country?

			not urgent						very urgent
C	4.1	Noise	1	2	3	4	5	6	7
C	4.2	Air pollution	1	2	3	4	5	6	7
C	4.3	Water pollution	1	2	3	4	5	6	7
C	4.4	Over population	1	2	3	4	5	6	7
C	4.5	Solid waste disposal	1	2	3	4	5	6	7
C	4.6	Toxic wastes	1	2	3	4	5	6	7
C	4.7	Nuclear wastes	1	2	3	4	5	6	7
C	4.8	Destruction of land and townscape	1	2	3	4	5	6	7
C	4.9	Depletion of natural resources (trees, minerals, wildlife)	1	2	3	4	5	6	7
C	4.10	Energy	1	2	3	4	5	6	7

In the next 10 years do you believe the following problems will get worse or be solved in this country?

			get worse						be solved
C	4.11	Noise	-3	-2	-1	0	1+	2+	3+
C	4.12	Air pollution	-3	-2	-1	0	1+	2+	3+
C	4.13	Water pollution	-3	-2	-1	0	1+	2+	3+
C	4.14	Over population	-3	-2	-1	0	1+	2+	3+
C	4.15	Solid waste disposal	-3	-2	-1	0	1+	2+	3+
C	4.16	Toxic wastes	-3	-2	-1	0	1+	2+	3+
C	4.17	Nuclear wastes	-3	-2	-1	0	1+	2+	3+
C	4.18	Destruction of land- and townscape	-3	-2	-1	0	1+	2+	3+
C	4.19	Depletion of natural resources	-3	-2	-1	0	1+	2+	3+
C	4.20	Energy	-3	-2	-1	0	1+	2+	3+

C 4.21 Do you think that the government's actions in dealing with environmental problems have been adequate?

      inadequate 1 2 3 4 5 6 7 adequate

4.22 Effective long range solution of environmental problems depends upon:

      changing our   ③ ② ① ⓪ ① ② ③   developing better
      lifestyle   technology

C 4.23 Please rank the following in terms of urgency for governmental action. (Put a number 1 in the box for the most urgent, ranking down to 6 for the least urgent.)

      a) ☐ social welfare (health, social security, education)
      b) ☐ law and order
      c) ☐ economy (inflation/unemployment)
      d) ☐ energy problems
      e) ☐ environmental problems
      f) ☐ foreign affairs

How much would you trust each of the following groups to solve environmental problems?

		no trust				great trust		
C 4.24	trade unions	1	2	3	4	5	6	7
C 4.25	environmental groups	1	2	3	4	5	6	7
C 4.26	government	1	2	3	4	5	6	7
C 4.27	political parties	1	2	3	4	5	6	7
C 4.28	industry	1	2	3	4	5	6	7
C 4.29	scientists and technologists	1	2	3	4	5	6	7
C 4.30	the general public	1	2	3	4	5	6	7

4.31   Which kind of change is <u>most</u> needed to solve our environmental problems?

greater scientific and technical development   [3] [2] [1] [0] [1] [2] [3]   basic change in the nature of society

4.32   Nature is OK but other things are more important.   [3] [2] [1] [0] [1] [2] [3]   I cherish nature and preserve it as one of the most precious things in life.

4.33   How much opportunity do you feel you have to influence environmental policy in your community?

none at all   1   2   3   4   5   6   7   very good opportunity

C 4.34   Our policy on national parks should:

guarantee access to all citizens   [3] [2] [1] [0] [1] [2] [3]   keep much land in a natural state accessible only by hiking

C 4.35   Generally speaking, how strongly do you favor or oppose the environmental movement?

strongly oppose   -3 -2 -1   0   1+ 2+ 3+   strongly favor

C 4.36   If the government planned to clean up pollution in your community, how strongly would you favor or oppose raising taxes for these projects knowing that your own taxes would go up?

strongly oppose   -3 -2 -1   0   1+ 2+ 3+   strongly favor

C 4.37   I perceive the condition of the environment as:

no problem   1   2   3   4   5   6   7   a large problem

C 4.38   How concerned are you about the environment?

not at all concerned   1   2   3   4   5   6   7   extremely concerned

C 4.39   Some people have suggested that protecting the environment could result in some people losing their jobs. Assuming that we have to settle for somewhat higher unemployment in order to protect the environment, is it more important to protect jobs or to protect the environment?

more important to protect jobs   [3] [2] [1] [0] [1] [2] [3]   more important to protect environment

C 4.40   How much change do you think will be necessary in our social, economic and political system in order to solve our environmental problems?

a) No basic change is needed to solve these problems.
b) A considerable amount of change is needed to solve these problems.
c) A completely new system is needed.
d) Change is needed but it's unattainable.
e) There is no environmental problem.

C 4.41   What is your attitude towards taking direct action (e.g. marches, demonstrations) in order to influence government decisions on issues such as airport sites, nuclear power stations, roads?

strongly oppose   1   2   3   4   5   6   7   strongly support

The following are some opposite opinions about the direction in which this country <u>should be</u> moving today. <u>Please circle a numbered box</u> on the scale indicating how strongly you prefer one direction or the other for our country.

5.1 A country that emphasizes allowing owners of land to use their property as they wish.   ③ ② ① ⓪ ① ② ③   A country that makes sure that private property is used in such a way that it benefits and does not injure the community.

5.2 A country that encourages people to remake their environment to suit their needs.   ③ ② ① ⓪ ① ② ③   A country that encourages people to adapt to their natural environment.

5.3 A country that saves its resources to benefit future generations.   ③ ② ① ⓪ ① ② ③   A country that uses its resources to benefit the present generation.

5.4 A country which believes economic growth is more important that protecting the environment.   ③ ② ① ⓪ ① ② ③   A country which believes protecting the environment is more important than economic growth.

5.5 A country which is willing to put up with some delay in order to let more people have a say in the big decisions.   ③ ② ① ⓪ ① ② ③   A country which is willing to let a few people make the big decisions in order to get things done quickly.

5.6 A country that emphasizes competition.   ③ ② ① ⓪ ① ② ③   A country that emphasizes cooperation.

5.7 A country that emphasizes preserving nature for its own sake.   ③ ② ① ⓪ ① ② ③   A country that emphasizes using nature to produce the goods we use.

5.8 A country that gets the energy it needs by better insulating its homes, driving cars that use less gasoline, and conserving more energy.   ③ ② ① ⓪ ① ② ③   A country that gets the energy it needs by digging more coal mines and drilling more oil wells, building more power plants, and producing more energy.

5.9 A country that uses taxes to insure that public goods (parks, clean air, recreation facilities, etc.) are well provided.   ③ ② ① ⓪ ① ② ③   A country that minimizes taxes, paying individuals maximum personal incomes.

C 6.1 Sex

    a) female

    b) male

C 6.2 Age

    a) under 21
    b) 21 - 30
    c) 31 - 40
    d) 41 - 50
    e) 51 - 60
    f) 61 - 70
    g) 71 and over

C 6.3 Marital status

    a) never married
    b) married
    c) divorced or separated
    d) widowed
    e) other

6.4 What kind of job do you do?

    a) professional, technical
    b) manager, administrator
    c) sales, clerical, craftsperson
    d) farmer, farm manager
    e) machine operators (including transportation)
    f) laborer
    g) service worker (including houseperson)
    h) student
    i) other _____(please write in)
    j) not employed

6.5 What kind of place do you work for?

    a) Agriculture, Forestry, Fishing
    b) Mining, Construction
    c) Manufacturing
    d) Transportation, Communications, Electric, Gas, Sanitary Services
    e) Wholesale and/or Retail Trade
    f) Finance, Insurance, Real Estate
    g) Government
    h) Education
    i) Services (including housewife)
    j) Other _____(please write in)
    k) Not employed

6.6 Does anyone in your immediate family belong to a trade union?

    a) no
    b) yes

6.7 I think of myself as belonging to

    a) the working class
    b) the lower middle class
    c) the upper middle class
    d) the upper class

6.8 Race

    a) black
    b) oriental
    c) American Indian
    d) white
    e) hispanic (Spanish speaking)
    f) other

C 6.9 Place where you grew up

    a) urban
    b) suburban
    c) small town
    d) rural

C 6.10 Your present home - permanent address

       a) urban
       b) suburban
       c) small town
       d) rural

C 6.11 Number of years of formal education

       a) 0 - 8 years
       b) 9 - 11 years
       c) 12 years (finished high school)
       d) 13 - 15 years
       e) 16 years (finished college)
       f) 17 + years

C 6.12 Total yearly family income

       a) less than $5,000
       b) $5,000 to $9,999
       c) 10,000 to 14,999
       d) 15,000 to 19,999
       e) 20,000 to 24,999
       f) 25,000 to 29,999
       g) 30,000 to 34,999
       h) over $35,000

C 6.13 What is your general political leaning?

       a) strong conservative
       b) moderate conservative
       c) middle of the road
       d) moderate liberal
       e) strong liberal

6.14 If an election were being held today, which party would get your support?

       a) definitely the Democrats
       b) probably the Democrats
       c) neither party
       d) probably the Republicans
       e) definitely the Republicans
       f) I wouldn't vote

C 6.15 Would you be influenced in your choice of party at the next election by its policy on environmental questions?

       a) probably
       b) possibly
       c) undecided
       d) no

C 6.16 Would you go so far as to vote for a party which would not normally get your support because of its policy on environmental issues?

       a) probably   c) undecided
       b) possibly   d) no

6.17 Generally speaking, do you usually think of yourself as:

       a) strong Democrat   e) Independent leaning Republican
       b) not so strong Democrat   f) not so strong Republican
       c) Independent leaning Democrat   g) strong Republican
       d) Independent

INTERNATIONAL ENVIRONMENT SURVEY

(How to fill out this questionnaire)

Did you fill out our questionnaire   ☐ yes
two years ago?   ☐ no

    This questionnaire primarily seeks your opinion. There are no right or
wrong answers. It will be apparent that many questions deal with the environment.
Please don't tell us what you think we want to hear. These are complicated problems with conflicting values. Please tell us what you really think.

    As you know, the same word can mean different things to different people;
hence, it is impossible to find a general wording to exactly suit every person.
Please bear with us if the wording of an item doesn't seem quite right to you
from time to time and do your best to answer the question. We hope we have gotten
the wording "right" for you most of the time.

    Please pay close attention to the directions for each part of the ques-
tionnaire. Generally, you will indicate your response by marking an X in the
box of your choice.

    For example, some questions ask you to choose between opposing views:

    I prefer warm weather | 3 |⊠| 1 | 0 | 1 | 2 | 3 | I prefer cold weather

    If you strongly prefer one or the other you would mark | 3 |. If you have no
preference, can't decide, or don't know, you would mark a | 0 |. If you have a
slight preference you would mark a | 1 | or a | 2 | depending on the strength of your
preference. Other items will use other kinds of scales which are self-evident.
In each case mark one response.

Many thanks for your help!

                Here are a number of statements about society and
                the environment. Please mark the numbered box that
                comes closest to expressing the extent of your agree-
                ment or disagreement with the item.

                                        strongly   strongly
                                        disagree   agree

C 1.1 There are likely to be serious and dis- | 1 | 2 | 3 | 4 | 5 | 6 | 7 |
      ruptive shortages of essential raw
      materials if things go on as they are.

C 1.2 The storage of nuclear wastes is too | 1 | 2 | 3 | 4 | 5 | 6 | 7 |
      dangerous.

C 1.3 Industrial societies provide a high | 1 | 2 | 3 | 4 | 5 | 6 | 7 |
      level of well-being for most people who
      live in them.

C 1.4 We are approaching the limit of the | 1 | 2 | 3 | 4 | 5 | 6 | 7 |
      number of people the earth can support.

C 1.5 A nuclear accident resulting in the | 1 | 2 | 3 | 4 | 5 | 6 | 7 |
      contamination of the environment is
      increasingly likely.

C 1.6 The good effects of technology outweigh | 1 | 2 | 3 | 4 | 5 | 6 | 7 |
      its bad effects.

C 1.7 We are fast using up the world's oil | 1 | 2 | 3 | 4 | 5 | 6 | 7 |
      resources.

C 1.8 Humans must live in harmony with | 1 | 2 | 3 | 4 | 5 | 6 | 7 |
      nature in order to survive.

C 1.9 We need nuclear power. | 1 | 2 | 3 | 4 | 5 | 6 | 7 |

C 1.10 Science and technology are our best | 1 | 2 | 3 | 4 | 5 | 6 | 7 |
       hope for the future.

C 1.11 Economically disruptive energy shortages | 1 | 2 | 3 | 4 | 5 | 6 | 7 |
       are likely to become more frequent if
       we go on as we are.

C 1.12 There are limits to growth beyond | 1 | 2 | 3 | 4 | 5 | 6 | 7 |
       which our industrialized society
       cannot expand.

C 1.13 We are being involved less and less in | 1 | 2 | 3 | 4 | 5 | 6 | 7 |
       important decisions which shape our lives.

C 1.14 We are in danger of letting technology run away with us.

| 1 | 2 | 3 | 4 | 5 | 6 | 7 |

C 1.15 Pollution is rising to dangerous levels.

| 1 | 2 | 3 | 4 | 5 | 6 | 7 |

C 1.16 The balance of nature is very delicate and easily upset.

| 1 | 2 | 3 | 4 | 5 | 6 | 7 |

C 1.17 Mankind is severely abusing the environment.

| 1 | 2 | 3 | 4 | 5 | 6 | 7 |

The following are contrasting statements about emphases or directions our society should be taking. Please mark the box with the number indicating the extent of your preference for one or the other emphasis:

C 2.1 A society that emphasizes economic growth.

| 3 | 2 | 1 | 0 | 1 | 2 | 3 |

A society that limits economic growth.

C 2.2 A society that emphasizes preserving nature for its own sake.

| 3 | 2 | 1 | 0 | 1 | 2 | 3 |

A society that emphasizes using nature to produce the goods we use.

C 2.3 A society which attaches relatively less importance to law and order.

| 3 | 2 | 1 | 0 | 1 | 2 | 3 |

A society which attaches relatively more importance to law and order.

C 2.4 A society that plans to avoid physical risks in the production of wealth.

| 3 | 2 | 1 | 0 | 1 | 2 | 3 |

A society that recognizes that physical risks are unavoidable in the production of wealth.

C 2.5 A society that emphasizes economic rewards for initiative and achievement.

| 3 | 2 | 1 | 0 | 1 | 2 | 3 |

A society that ensures a minimum standard of living for everyone.

C 2.6 A society which emphasizes work which is humanly satisfying.

| 3 | 2 | 1 | 0 | 1 | 2 | 3 |

A society where work is controlled mainly by economic needs.

C 2.7 A society that emphasizes foresight and planning by government for the public good.

| 3 | 2 | 1 | 0 | 1 | 2 | 3 |

A society that relies on the supply and demand market to maximize the public good.

C 2.8 A society with many chances for citizens to take part in political decisions.

| 3 | 2 | 1 | 0 | 1 | 2 | 3 |

A society with few chances for citizens to take part in political decisions.

C 2.9 A society which financially rewards differences in skill, education and achievement.

| 3 | 2 | 1 | 0 | 1 | 2 | 3 |

A society which emphasizes similar incomes for everyone.

C 2.10 A society in which people are judged mainly by their personal qualities.

| 3 | 2 | 1 | 0 | 1 | 2 | 3 |

A society in which people are judged mainly by their achievements.

C 2.11 A society in which there is an emphasis on rules.

| 3 | 2 | 1 | 0 | 1 | 2 | 3 |

A society in which there is an emphasis on individual judgement.

C 2.12 A society that emphasizes environmental protection over economic growth.

| 3 | 2 | 1 | 0 | 1 | 2 | 3 |

A society that emphasizes economic growth over environmental protection.

C 2.13 A society which is willing to put up with some delay in order to let more people have a say in the big decisions.

| 3 | 2 | 1 | 0 | 1 | 2 | 3 |

A society which is willing to let a few people make the big decisions in order to get things done quickly.

C 2.14 A society in which people have responsibility to protect themselves from harm.

| 3 | 2 | 1 | 0 | 1 | 2 | 3 |

A society in which the government has responsibility to protect people from harm.

C 2.15 A society that saves its resources to benefit future generations.

| 3 | 2 | 1 | 0 | 1 | 2 | 3 |

A society that uses its resources to benefit the present generation.

Please answer the following questions by marking the appropriate box.

C 3.1 Have you ever belonged to a nature conservation association?

no, not interested [1]   yes, past member/not current member [3]
no, but interested [2]   yes, current member, but not active [4]
                          yes, currently active member [5]

C 3.2 Have you ever belonged to an environmental/ecology group?

no, not interested [1]   yes, past member / not current member [3]
no, but interested [2]   yes, current member, but nbt active [4]
                          yes, currently active member [5]

C 3.3 Have you ever complained about an environmental problem to someone in authority?

never [1]
yes, once [2]
yes, more than once [3]

How urgent are the following environmental problems?

	not urgent						very urgent
4.1 noise	1	2	3	4	5	6	7
4.2 air pollution	1	2	3	4	5	6	7
4.3 water pollution	1	2	3	4	5	6	7
4.4 over-population	1	2	3	4	5	6	7
4.5 solid waste disposal	1	2	3	4	5	6	7
4.6 toxic wastes	1	2	3	4	5	6	7
4.7 nuclear wastes	1	2	3	4	5	6	7
4.8 destruction of land- and townscape	1	2	3	4	5	6	7
4.9 depletion of natural resources (trees, minerals, wildlife)	1	2	3	4	5	6	7
4.10 energy	1	2	3	4	5	6	7

C In the next ten years, do you believe the following problems will get worse or get better?

	get worse						get better
4.11 noise	1	2	3	4	5	6	7
4.12 air pollution	1	2	3	4	5	6	7
4.13 water pollution	1	2	3	4	5	6	7
4.14 over-population	1	2	3	4	5	6	7
4.15 solid waste disposal	1	2	3	4	5	6	7
4.16 toxic wastes	1	2	3	4	5	6	7
4.17 nuclear wastes	1	2	3	4	5	6	7
4.18 destruction of land- and townscape	1	2	3	4	5	6	7
4.19 depletion of natural resources (trees, minerals, wildlife)	1	2	3	4	5	6	7
4.20 energy	1	2	3	4	5	6	7

	low						high
4.21 How is the quality of the environment where you live?	1	2	3	4	5	6	7

	inadequate						adequate
4.22 Do you think that governmental actions in dealing with environmental problems have been adequate?	1	2	3	4	5	6	7

4.23 Would you be willing to pay more taxes to protect the environment?

yes, I am willing to pay this much more per yr. | $ |
no, I am not willing to pay more | 2 |
I am undecided | 3 |

Is the amount of tax money that government is spending on each of the following problems too little, about right, or too much?

	too little						too much
4.24 defense	1	2	3	4	5	6	7
4.25 public security (police, courts, etc.)	1	2	3	4	5	6	7
4.26 primary and secondary education	1	2	3	4	5	6	7
4.27 higher education (college, universities)	1	2	3	4	5	6	7
4.28 health care	1	2	3	4	5	6	7
4.29 sport and recreation	1	2	3	4	5	6	7
4.30 housing	1	2	3	4	5	6	7
4.31 environmental protection	1	2	3	4	5	6	7
4.32 assistance to trade and industry	1	2	3	4	5	6	7
4.33 transportation (roads, public transport)	1	2	3	4	5	6	7
4.34 public utilities (power, water, etc.)	1	2	3	4	5	6	7
4.35 development aid to the developing countries	1	2	3	4	5	6	7
4.36 support of arts and culture	1	2	3	4	5	6	7
4.37 development of new energy sources	1	2	3	4	5	6	7

How much would you trust each of the following groups to solve environmental problems?

	no trust						great trust
4.41 trade unions	1	2	3	4	5	6	7
4.42 environmental action groups	1	2	3	4	5	6	7
4.43 government	1	2	3	4	5	6	7
4.44 political parties	1	2	3	4	5	6	7
4.45 industry	1	2	3	4	5	6	7
4.46 scientists and technologists	1	2	3	4	5	6	7
4.47 the general public	1	2	3	4	5	6	7
4.48 nature conservation associations	1	2	3	4	5	6	7

4.49 Which kind of change is most needed to solve our environmental problems?

greater scientific and technical development | 3 | 2 | 1 | 0 | 1 | 2 | 3 | basic change in the nature of society

4.50 Nature is OK but other things are more important. | 3 | 2 | 1 | 0 | 1 | 2 | 3 | I cherish nature and preserve it as one of the most precious things in life.

Do you think that your contact with the natural environment is too little, about right, or too much...

	too little						too much
4.51 in the course of your working day	1	2	3	4	5	6	7
4.52 in your leisure time	1	2	3	4	5	6	7
4.53 on holiday	1	2	3	4	5	6	7

How much influence do you have as a result of your own efforts and activities, over the following areas of your daily life:

	little						much
4.61 environment at your place of residence	1	2	3	4	5	6	7
4.62 local political decisions	1	2	3	4	5	6	7
4.63 regional and national political decisions	1	2	3	4	5	6	7
4.64 work life	1	2	3	4	5	6	7
4.65 private life	1	2	3	4	5	6	7

C

C 4.66 How active are you in trying to influence environmental policy in your community?

not at all | 1 | 2 | 3 | 4 | 5 | 6 | 7 | very active

C 4.71 Generally speaking, how strongly do you favor or oppose the environmental movement?

strongly oppose | 1 | 2 | 3 | 4 | 5 | 6 | 7 | strongly favor

C 4.72 I perceive the condition of the world environment as:

no problem | 1 | 2 | 3 | 4 | 5 | 6 | 7 | large problem

C 4.73 Some people have suggested that protecting the environment could result in some people losing their jobs. Assuming that we have to settle for somewhat higher unemployment in order to protect the environment, is it more important to protect jobs or to protect the environment?

more important to protect jobs | 3 | 2 | 1 | 0 | 1 | 2 | 3 | more important to protect the environment

C 4.74 What is your attitude towards taking direct action (e.g., marches, demonstrations) in order to influence government decisions on issues such as airport sites, nuclear power stations, roads?

strongly oppose | 1 | 2 | 3 | 4 | 5 | 6 | 7 | strongly support

C 4.75 Generally speaking, how strongly do you favor or oppose the peace movement (those who openly oppose weapons buildup)?

strongly oppose | 1 | 2 | 3 | 4 | 5 | 6 | 7 | strongly favor

4.76 Effective long range solution of environmental problems depends upon:

changing our lifestyle | 3 | 2 | 1 | 0 | 1 | 2 | 3 | developing better technology

4.77 If the government planned to clean up pollution in your community, how strongly would you favor or oppose raising taxes for these projects knowing that your own taxes would go up?

strongly oppose | 1 | 2 | 3 | 4 | 5 | 6 | 7 | strongly favor

The following are some opposite opinions about the direction in which this country should be moving today. Please mark a numbered box on the scale indicating how strongly you prefer one direction or the other for our country.

5.1 A country that emphasizes allowing owners of land to use their property as they wish. | 3 | 2 | 1 | 0 | 1 | 2 | 3 | A country that makes sure that private property is used in such a way that it benefits and does not injure the community.

5.2 A country that encourages people to remake their environment to suit their needs. | 3 | 2 | 1 | 0 | 1 | 2 | 3 | A country that encourages people to adapt to their natural environment.

5.3 A country that emphasizes competition. | 3 | 2 | 1 | 0 | 1 | 2 | 3 | A country that emphasizes cooperation.

5.4 A country that gets the energy it needs by better insulating its homes, driving cars that use less gasoline, and conserving more energy. | 3 | 2 | 1 | 0 | 1 | 2 | 3 | A country that gets the energy it needs by digging more coal mines and drilling more oil wells, building more power plants, and producing more energy.

5.5 A country that uses taxes to insure that public goods (parks, clean air, recreation facilities, etc.) are well provided. | 3 | 2 | 1 | 0 | 1 | 2 | 3 | A country that minimizes taxes, paying individuals maximum personal incomes.

5.6 A country that emphasizes using resources from public (government owned) lands for industrial/economic purposes.

3	2	1	0	1	2	3

A country that emphasizes preserving public lands as national parks, forests, etc., in order to save the natural environment.

5.7 A country where people believe that considerable governmental regulation is required to protect the environment.

3	2	1	0	1	2	3

A country where people believe that little government regulation is required to protect the environment.

How often do you obtain information on environmental problems from the following sources?

	never						often
C 5.8 Newspapers, magazines	1	2	3	4	5	6	7
C 5.9 Television/radio	1	2	3	4	5	6	7
C 5.10 Discussion with family/friends	1	2	3	4	5	6	7
C 5.11 Discussion with people at work	1	2	3	4	5	6	7
C 5.12 Books, journals	1	2	3	4	5	6	7
C 5.13 Lectures, meetings	1	2	3	4	5	6	7
C 5.14 Special publicity by interested groups	1	2	3	4	5	6	7

5.15 "Congress is reconsidering the Clean Air Act, which is now ten years old. Given the costs involved in cleaning up the environment, do you think Congress should make the Clean Air Act stricter than it is now, keep it about the same, or make it less strict?"

Make it stricter [1]   Make it less strict [3]

Keep about the same [2]   Not sure [4]

5.16 "The Clean Air Act does not permit the consideration of costs when setting standards for the protection of human health. The Reagan Administration is considering asking Congress to require that pollution standards designed to protect human health be relaxed if the costs are too high. Do you favor or oppose relaxing pollution standards affecting human health if the costs are too high?

Favor relaxing standards [1]

Oppose relaxing standards [2]

Not sure [3]

Here are some questions about yourself. Please mark the appropriate box or fill in the answer where required.

C 6.1 sex:
female [1]
male [2]

C 6.2 Please write your age in the boxes
☐☐ years

C 6.3 marital status:
never married [1]
living together [2]
married [3]
divorced/separated [4]
widowed [5]

C 6.4 occupation: (even if retired, your main occupation)

manual, unskilled and semi-skilled	1
skilled manual, clerical, sales, personal services	2
supervisor, inspector	3
manager, administration, executive	4
self-employed businessman (includes farmer)	5
professional/technical	6
household worker (housespouse)	7
student	8
not employed	9

C 6.5 If working, in which sector?

manufacturing, construction, industry	1
commerce (transport, banking, insurance, trade, etc)	2
health, welfare	3
education, science	4
other public services/administration	5
other service workers	6
media, entertainment, arts, etc.	7
agriculture, forestry, fishing, mining	8
household service	9

6.6 Are you a member of a trade union?

yes	1
no	2

C 6.7 I think of myself as:

working class	1
lower middle class	2
upper middle class	3
upper class	4

C 6.8 Your present home (permanent) address:

urban	1
suburban	2
small town	3
rural	4

6.9 Number of years of formal education

0 - 8 years	1
9 - 11 years	2
12 years (finished high school)	3
13 - 15 years	4
16 years (finished college)	5
17 + years	6

C 6.10 Total yearly family income **for all income earners in your household**

less than $5,000	1
$5,000 to $9,999	2
$10,000 to $14,999	3
$15,000 to $19,999	4
$20,000 to $24,999	5
$25,000 to $29,999	6
$30,000 to $34,999	7
$35,000 to $44,999	8
$45,000 or more	9

C 6.11 How many persons depend on this income?

☐☐ persons

C 6.12 What is your general political leaning?

strong conservative	1
moderate conservative	2
middle of the road	3
moderate liberal	4
strong liberal	5
no position	8

6.13 If an election were being held today, which party would get your support:

definitely the Republicans	1
probably the Republicans	2
neither party	3
probably the Democrats	4
definitely the Democrats	5
I wouldn't vote	6

C 6.14 Would you be influenced in your choice of party at the next election by its policy on environmental questions?

probably	1
possibly	2
undecided	3
no	4

6.15 What state do you live in? _____

Write in name of state

5.16 Race

black	1
oriental	2
American Indian	3
white	4
hispanic (Spanish speaking)	5
other	6

Appendix C

TABLE C-1
Levels of Support For Environmental Values in the U.S. Public in 1980–1982*

Item	% Disagreeing/Rejecting Environmental Perspective		% Agreeing/Accepting Environmental Perspective	
	1980	1982	1980	1982
1. There are likely to be serious and disruptive shortages of essential raw materials if things go on as they are.	10	18	88	69
2. The storage of nuclear wastes is too dangerous.	24	23	66	66
3. Humans must live in harmony with nature in order to survive.	6	8	92	87
4. Mankind is severely abusing the environment.	14	17	80	76
5. A society that emphasizes environmental protection over economic growth.	19	21	62	59
6. A society that saves its resources to benefit future generations rather than using them for the present generation.	16	14	73	73
7. Nature is OK but other things are more important vs. I cherish nature and preserve it as one of the most precious things in life.	16	14	73	76
8. Generally speaking, how strongly do you favor or oppose the environmental movement?	17	19	67	53
9. I perceive the condition of the world environment to be a large problem.	15	8	62	76
10. A country that encourages people to remake their environment to suit their needs vs. a country that encourages people to adapt to their natural environment.	17	15	73	71
11. A country that gets the energy it needs by better insulating its homes, driving cars that use less gasoline, and conserving more energy vs. a country that gets the energy it needs by digging more coal mines and drilling more oil wells, building more power plants, and producing more energy.	19	12	71	77
12. Environmental problems are urgent. (an average across 10 problems)	14	15	70	72

* Persons taking a neutral position on these questions are not reported in the table; hence, the percentages will not add to 100.

TABLE C-2
A Society That Emphasizes
(Percentage in each Response Category)

	Preserving Nature for its Own Sake				Using Nature to Produce the Goods We Use			
	3	2	1	0	1	2	3	Mean*
United States 1980								
General Public	12	12	16	14	19	12	14	4.15
Environmentalists	32	28	18	12	5	1	2	2.40
Business Leaders	3	5	16	12	27	21	14	4.74
Labor Leaders	11	12	10	19	19	12	17	4.27
Elected Officials	3	7	25	24	18	19	4	4.17
Appointed Officials	5	10	22	15	29	16	3	3.98
Media Gatekeepers	6	16	28	16	26	6	2	3.66
United States 1982								
General Public	17	15	13	11	11	15	18	4.01
Environmentalists	30	26	14	10	6	7	5	2.77
Business Leaders	5	7	10	14	22	24	18	4.85
Labor Leaders	14	19	11	11	16	14	15	3.98
Elected Officials	7	13	29	13	13	11	13	4.34
Appointed Officials	6	18	17	11	23	16	9	3.84
Germany 1982								
General Public	32	16	9	6	8	14	16	3.43
Environmentalists	34	23	12	10	8	7	6	2.79
Business Leaders	15	10	12	5	20	23	15	4.34
Members of Parliament	7	17	19	11	17	19	10	4.12
England 1982								
General Public	23	12	10	9	12	15	19	3.94
Environmentalists	28	19	18	12	8	9	6	3.02
Business Leaders	9	15	10	14	17	21	14	4.32
Public Officials	12	13	12	24	16	12	11	4.01

* The scale positions were coded 1-7 from left to right for data analysis. The mean score for each group is based on that numerical scale.

TABLE C.3
A Society That Emphasizes:
(Percentage in each response category)

	Environmental protection over economic growth.								Economic growth over environmental protection.			
	3		2		1		0		1			Mean	Mean
	80	82	80	82	80	82	80	82	80	82		80	82

	3 80	3 82	2 80	2 82	1 80	1 82	0 80	0 82	1 80	1 82	2 80	2 82	3 80	3 82	Mean 80	Mean 82
United States																
General Public	26	21	18	21	18	17	19	20	8	9	5	7	6	5	2.99	3.17
Environmentalists	52	45	24	27	8	12	12	12	1	1	1	3	2	1	1.97	2.12
Business Leaders	8	5	5	7	16	8	30	30	28	29	6	14	8	7	4.16	4.40
Labor Leaders	20	23	18	14	13	17	29	26	5	12	8	3	6	5	3.26	3.16
Appointed Officials	12	5	15	19	21	17	34	34	11	17	7	8	1	0	3.45	3.62
Elected Officials	5	13	19	17	23	17	32	36	12	9	5	4	4	4	3.58	3.40
Media Gatekeepers	11	—	15	—	24	—	29	—	17	—	1	—	4	—	3.48	—
United Kingdom																
General Public	29	28	19	24	18	11	22	16	6	8	2	6	4	7	2.80	2.955
Conservation Society (same as Environmentalists in 82)	66	57	25	27	3	9	5	4	1	2	0	1	0	0	1.48	1.70
Nature Conservationists	44	—	23	—	15	—	13	—	2	—	2	—	2	—	2.18	—
Business Leaders	13	10	15	18	20	17	37	35	10	12	3	6	3	3	3.38	3.49
Labor Leaders	28	—	14	—	19	—	26	—	5	—	4	—	4	—	2.95	—
Public Officials	13	14	19	19	25	22	27	29	11	8	3	6	3	1	3.23	3.22
Germany																
General Public	38	31	13	13	9	11	18	13	6	8	5	12	11	12	2.99	3.38
Environmentalists	56	61	20	14	5	5	6	5	4	3	3	7	6	5	2.16	2.14
Business Leaders	17	7	14	14	11	14	31	29	15	19	9	15	4	2	3.55	3.92
Public Officials	26	13	22	22	9	18	28	28	9	10	4	6	1	3	2.88	3.28

TABLE C.4
A Country That:
(Percentages by response category)

	Saves it resources to benefit future generations.						Uses its resources to benefit the present generation.	
	3	2	1	0	1	2	3	Mean*
United States 1980								
General Public	29	22	22	13	7	4	5	2.78
Environmentalists	48	30	10	6	1	2	2	1.99
Business Leaders	16	25	18	25	12	3	1	3.09
Labor Leaders	30	21	18	19	5	2	5	2.74
Appointed Officials	15	28	31	18	4	3	1	2.81
Elected Officials	23	21	23	25	4	1	3	2.81
Media Gatekeepers	18	21	31	16	9	3	2	2.94
United States 1982								
General Public	31	26	16	14	6	4	4	2.62
Environmentalists	48	27	12	7	2	3	1	2.03
Business Leaders	16	19	19	25	11	7	3	3.28
Labor Leaders	27	27	18	16	8	2	2	2.65
Appointed Officials	12	34	22	23	7	1	2	2.90
Elected Officials	11	20	17	13	17	15	7	3.78
Germany 1982								
General Public	42	18	9	6	5	9	11	2.82
Environmentalists	71	9	6	2	3	4	5	2.03
Business Leaders	35	28	18	1	9	8	2	2.53
Members of Parliament	39	29	16	6	6	6	0	2.27
England 1982								
General Public	31	21	15	12	7	4	10	2.95
Environmentalists	52	30	10	6	1	0	1	1.76
Business Leaders	18	25	23	21	8	4	2	2.94
Public Officials	21	22	19	26	8	4	1	2.92

* The scale positions were coded 1–7 from left to right for data analysis. The mean score for each group is based on that numerical scale.

TABLE C-5
A Society That:
(Percentage in each response category, 1982)

	Plans to avoid physical risks in the production of wealth				Recognizes that risks are unavoidable in the production of wealth			
	3	2	1	0	1	2	3	Mean
United States								
Environmentalists	28	24	13	10	13	7	4	2.97
General Public	21	20	13	13	13	12	9	3.48
Labor Leaders	32	17	9	5	16	13	7	3.26
Appointed Officials	9	19	17	5	27	18	5	3.96
Elected Officials	26	17	19	2	21	9	6	3.28
Business Leaders	7	8	11	4	21	29	20	4.92
England								
Conservation Society	40	20	12	11	8	5	4	2.56
General Public	33	17	8	8	10	14	9	3.24
Public Officials	19	16	12	12	22	11	9	3.69
Business Leaders	11	15	11	11	17	18	17	4.26
Germany								
Environmentalists	56	15	9	4	3	9	5	2.28
General Public	33	17	11	6	9	12	13	3.27
Public Officials	17	26	17	6	17	14	5	3.40
Business Leaders	15	20	13	8	22	14	9	3.79

TABLE C-6
What Kind of Change is Most Needed
to Solve Our Environmental Problems?

	Greater Scientific and Technical Development						Basic Change in Nature of Society	
	3	2	1	0	1	2	3	Mean*
United States 1980								
General Public	18	10	9	11	13	13	25	4.47
Environmentalists	5	3	6	14	14	19	39	5.42
Business Leaders	40	23	7	7	8	6	7	2.46
Labor Leaders	40	13	1	8	8	10	19	3.37
Elected Officials	15	13	13	11	25	11	11	4.11
Appointed Officials	16	18	12	13	20	11	11	3.79
Media Gatekeepers	20	16	14	14	14	9	14	3.68
United States 1982								
General Public	12	9	9	11	14	19	26	4.85
Environmentalists	7	8	5	10	13	23	35	5.21
Business Leaders	33	21	13	9	8	8	8	2.94
Labor Leaders	22	13	11	8	12	16	18	3.99
Elected Officials	15	24	4	13	13	20	11	3.89
Appointed Officials	17	24	10	10	11	19	8	3.64
Germany 1982								
General Public	29	13	6	9	6	13	25	3.88
Environmentalists	14	5	3	7	6	19	46	5.27
Business Leaders	52	21	6	6	4	6	5	2.27
Members of Parliament	32	16	7	10	11	12	12	3.36
England 1982								
General Public	8	11	6	9	11	17	37	5.04
Environmentalists	3	2	4	6	13	22	50	5.88
Business Leaders	15	16	12	10	16	17	15	4.06
Public Officials	7	21	9	13	16	13	21	4.34

* The scale positions were coded 1–7 from left to right for data analysis. The mean score for each group is based on that numerical scale.

TABLE C-7

Need for Social Change

"How much change do you think will be necessary in our social, economic and political system in order to solve our environmental problems?" (Percentage in each response category)

General Public and Leader Groups/Each Country	(n)	there is no problem	no basic change needed	considerable change needed	completely new system	change needed but unattainable
United States						
Environmentalists	225	0%	4%	80%	10%	5%
General Public	1513	1	10	65	16	8
Labor Leaders	85	1	16	62	10	11
Appointed Officials	153	1	21	63	6	9
Elected Officials	78	1	24	62	10	3
Media Gatekeepers	105	1	27	61	2	10
Business Leaders	223	1	34	50	5	11
England						
Conservation Society	176	0	5	67	24	3
Nature Conservationists	200	1	12	64	14	10
General Public	725	1	11	52	25	11
Labor Leaders	308	0	9	50	34	7
Public Officials	188	1	34	54	5	6
Business Leaders	261	0	26	53	12	9
Germany						
Environmentalists	98	0	6	70	20	2
General Public	1088	2	16	59	9	13
Public Officials	102	0	24	62	2	12
Business Leaders	130	3	38	52	0	6

TABLE C-8

Percentage Taking Environmentally Protective Actions by Group for Each Country
1980

General Public and Leader Groups/Each Country	regularly separate rubbish	consider packaging	participate environmental issues	belong environmental groups	belong nature conservation associations	likely to complain
United States						
Environmentalists	47	27	70	90	77	42
General Public	23	21	17	10	14	34
Labor Leaders	28	24	33	20	18	58
Appointed Officials	29	13	39	29	25	46
Elected Officials	18	3	62	39	27	68
Media Gatekeepers	33	9	35	16	22	52
Business Leaders	18	6	23	18	29	29
England						
Conservation Society	67	32	64	87	69	53
Nature Conservationists	62	21	45	44	97	48
General Public	33	20	15	12	13	50
Labor Leaders	42	17	33	15	11	68
Public Officials	45	12	27	24	38	61
Business Leaders	28	8	27	21	31	55
Germany						
Environmentalists	85	56	70	53	71	89
General Public	67	43	10	3	7	64
Public Officials	78	27	45	3	16	80
Business Leaders	72	31	14	1	16	74
Publics						
U.S. Public	23	21	17	10	14	34
English Public	33	20	15	12	13	50
German Public	67	43	10	3	7	64

TABLE C-9
What is Your General Political Leaning? (USA)
How Would You Estimate Yourself Politically? (England)
Wie Würden Sie Ihre Politische Einstellung Einschätzen? (Germany)

General Public and Leader Groups/Each Country	strong liberal left		middle left		center		middle right		strong conservative right		no position	
	80	82	80	82	80	82	80	82	80	82	80	82
United States	%	%	%	%	%	%	%	%	%	%	%	%
Environmentalists*	23	24	41	43	13	14	20	15	2	2		2
General Public	2	3	18	17	42	27	33	34	5	7		11
Labor Leaders	18	32	44	42	17	12	21	10	0	3		1
Appointed Officials	5	5	36	37	19	16	36	37	4	4		2
Elected Officials	4	13	35	34	15	19	32	32	13	2		0
Media Gatekeepers	2	–	36	–	19	–	38	–	6	–		–
Business Leaders	0	0	11	12	18	16	60	59	11	11		1
England												
Conservation Society	17	12	30	35	21	17	17	20	5	8	9	8
Nature Conservationists	4	–	15	–	22	–	33	–	14	–	10	–
General Public	6	5	13	13	25	22	22	25	13	11	18	23
Labor Leaders	29	–	32	–	25	–	9	–	2	–	3	–
Public Officials	7	7	23	24	19	27	36	25	7	13	7	4
Business Leaders	2	1	6	6	20	23	48	46	22	21	3	3
Germany												
Environmentalists	9	22	27	32	29	18	15	11	3	1	14	17
General Public	3	3	16	17	39	33	23	24	6	6	12	17
Public Officials	3	15	34	34	37	39	14	13	1	0	9	0
Business Leaders	1	0	8	4	30	31	49	51	8	12	3	2

* To facilitate comparison with 1980, only the environmentalists falling in the panel are reported for 1982.

TABLE C-10
Would You Be Influenced in Your Choice of Party at the Next Election
by Its Policy on Environmental Questions?

General Public and Leader Groups/Each Country	no		undecided		possibly		probably	
	80	82	80	82	80	82	80	82
United States	%	%	%	%	%	%	%	%
Environmentalists	4	1	4	2	20	22	71	75
General Public	17	15	17	18	45	43	21	24
Labor Leaders	22	23	11	17	49	41	17	19
Appointed Officials	22	24	9	6	40	44	29	26
Elected Officials	30	43	10	4	41	30	19	23
Media Gatekeepers	16	–	9	–	45	–	30	–
Business Leaders	35	30	11	12	39	47	15	11
England								
Conservation Society	9	12	2	4	34	33	54	50
Nature Conservationists	18	–	7	–	46	–	29	–
General Public	31	32	15	16	36	34	18	19
Labor Leaders	57	–	3	–	26	–	14	–
Public Officials	49	42	4	5	33	37	14	16
Business Leaders	50	45	8	8	35	39	7	7
Germany (82 only)								
Environmentalists	–	17	–	4	–	15	–	64
General Public	–	34	–	12	–	33	–	21
Business Leaders	–	57	–	8	–	23	–	12

TABLE C-11
How Much Would You Trust Each of the Following Groups to Solve Environmental Problems?
(mean levels of trust)
1980**

General Public and Leader Groups/Each Country	Trade Unions	Environmental Groups	Government	Political Parties	Industry	Scientists & Technologists	General Public
United States							
Environmentalists	2.30	5.66*	3.52	2.24	2.14*	4.26*	3.74
General Public	2.14	4.54	3.45	2.23	3.06	5.04	3.73
Labor Leaders	4.71*	4.46	3.64	2.20	2.33	5.33	3.86
Appointed Officials	2.30	4.08	4.37*	2.85	3.16	5.00	3.89
Elected Officials	2.38	4.37	3.88	2.92*	3.08	4.76	4.05*
Media Gatekeepers	1.86	4.14	3.37	2.50	2.91	4.77	3.72
Business Leaders	1.69	3.35*	3.11	2.02	4.25*	5.39*	3.65
England							
Conservation Society	2.09	5.40*	2.92*	2.59	2.16*	3.84*	3.12
Nature Conservationists	1.73	5.08	3.84	2.87	2.94	4.29	3.21
General Public	2.33	4.81	3.57	2.97	3.17	4.74*	3.50*
Labor Leaders	4.46*	4.87	3.17	3.17	2.32	4.29	3.32
Public Officials	1.86	3.82*	3.96	2.86	2.90	4.15	3.11
Business Leaders	1.84	4.09	3.98	2.75	3.53*	4.33	3.27
Germany							
Environmentalists	2.30	6.10*	3.80*	3.19	2.67*	4.69*	3.86
General Public	2.59	5.73	4.78	3.92	3.12	5.17	4.00*
Public Officials	2.46	5.28	5.11*	4.37	3.53	5.46	3.86
Business Leaders	2.36	4.56	4.96	4.15	4.74*	5.82*	3.78
Publics							
USA Public	2.14	4.54	3.45	2.23	3.06	5.04*	3.73
English Public	2.33	4.81*	3.57	2.97	3.17	4.74	3.50
German Public	2.59	5.73*	4.78*	3.92*	3.12	5.17*	4.00
Environmentalists							
USA	2.30	5.66*	3.52	2.24	2.14	4.26	3.74
English Conservation Soc.	2.09	5.40*	2.92	2.59	2.16	3.84	3.12
Germany	2.30	6.10*	3.80	3.19	2.67	4.69	3.86
Business Leaders							
USA	1.69	3.35	3.11	2.02	4.25	5.39*	3.65
England	1.84	4.09	3.98	2.75	3.53	4.33*	3.27
Germany	2.36	4.56	4.96	4.15	4.74	5.82*	3.78

* Means to be especially noted for comparison.
** Careful scrutiny of the 1982 data disclose, by and large, no significant shift in these feelings of trust.

Appendix D

Correlation Matrix for Items in the **Environmentalism Scale**

	1	2	3	4	5
1. Generally speaking, how strongly do you favor or oppose the environmental movement? strongly oppose −3 −2 −1 0 1+ 2+ 3+ strongly favor	1.00				
2. If the government planned to clean up pollution in your community, how strongly would you favor or oppose raising taxes for these projects knowing that your own taxes would go up? strongly oppose −3 −2 −1 0 1+ 2+ 3+ strongly favor	.50	1.00			
3. I perceive the condition of the environment as: no problem 1 2 3 4 5 6 7 a large problem	.57	.49	1.00		
4. How concerned are you about the environment? not at all 1 2 3 4 5 6 7 extremely concerned concerned	.55	.47	.74	1.00	
5. Some people have suggested that protecting the environment could result in some people losing their jobs. Assuming that we have to settle for somewhat higher unemployment in order to protect the environment, is it more important to protect jobs or to protect the environment? more important to 3 2 1 0 1 2 3 more important to protect jobs protect environment	.47	.44	.51	.49	1.00

The **Environmental Behavior Index** is made up from answers to the following items:

3.9 Do you separate your household rubbish (e.g. glass, paper) for recycling?

never   always
1 2 3 4 5 6 7

3.11 Do you take into account the amount of packaging on goods when you buy?

never   always
1 2 3 4 5 6 7

3.12 Do you participate actively on environmental issues?

   a) no
   b) yes

3.13 Do you belong to any environmental groups?

   a) no
   b) yes, one or two
   c) yes, three or more

3.14 Do you belong to any nature conservation associations?

   a) no
   b) yes, one or two
   c) yes, three or more

3.16 How likely would you be to complain to someone in authority?

   a) not likely
   b) somewhat likely
   c) very likely

Post-Materialism Items used in the English Questionnaire

Here is a list of four possible aims for the country as a whole. What do you think this county's priorities should be for the next ten years or so?
Please put a 1 against the aim which you think is most desirable. Then put a 2 against the *next* most desirable aim and *leave the remaining two boxes blank.*

5.1	Maintaining a high rate of economic growth.	☐
5.2	Making sure that this country has a strong defence force.	☐
5.3	Seeing that the people have more say in how things get decided at work and in their communities.	☐
5.4	Protect nature from being spoiled and polluted.	☐

Now do the same for these four aims.
Please put a 1 against the aim which you think is most desirable. Then put a 2 against the next most desirable aim and *leave the remaining two boxes blank.*

5.5	Maintaining order in the nation.	☐
5.6	Giving the people more say in important government decisions.	☐
5.7	Fighting rising prices.	☐
5.8	Protecting freedom of speech.	☐

Now do the same for these four aims.
Please put a 1 against the aim which you think is most desirable. Then put a 2 against the next most desirable aim and *leave the remaining two boxes blank.*

5.9	Maintain a stable economy.	☐
5.10	Progress toward a less impersonal, more humane society.	☐
5.11	The fight against crime.	☐
5.12	Progress toward a society where ideas are more important than money.	☐

Appendix E

Description of the Three-Nation Study
of Environmental Beliefs and Values

History of the Study

The Environmental Studies Center at the State University of New York at Buffalo and the International Institute for Environment and Society (part of the Science Center in Berlin) had each developed, quite independently, a research program focusing on environmental beliefs and values. Each institution perceived that humans were redefining their relationship to nature and had chosen to study how that process was developing. These two institutions discovered each other, and their common interests, in the summer of 1978; the basic design of the study was agreed to in conference in Berlin that summer. Professor Stephen Cotgrove and his associates at the Science Studies Centre at the University of Bath in England had been conducting related studies so he was invited to join the project.

A meeting of the leaders of the three teams was convened at the University of Bath in England in February, 1979, to delineate the general outlines of the collaborative project and to prepare preliminary drafts of a research instrument. Pilot studies were conducted at the three institutions over the summer of 1979. These pilot studies utilized several hundred cases providing an excellent basis for judging which items to retain in the final questionnaire. Limited resources at each of the institutions dictated that we use mail questionnaires rather than personal interviews. This was not a decision that we took lightly since we were acutely aware of the problems and difficulties arising from the use of mail questionnaires (these will be discussed later). We adopted procedures to overcome many of those difficulties and are convinced, after careful examination of the data, that we have acquired a data set that can be very informative with respect to the social phenomena we desire to understand.

Fieldwork was undertaken in each of the three countries early in 1980 and was completed in late spring-early summer. Analysis of the data disclosed many interesting findings that we share with you in this book.

We had in mind all along the possibility of continuing the study on a longitudinal basis if the data from the first wave proved to be reliable, valid, and interesting. We believed that the phenomena we were trying to understand would be changing over time and that following those changes as closely as possible would enable us to better understand the dynamics of the process. We concluded in the summer of 1981 that we should continue the study longitudinally and planning began soon thereafter for the second wave. The second wave was completed in each of the three countries during the first half of 1982.

Sample Design

Since we were studying the process by which societies change their beliefs about their relationship to nature, we wished to study relevant environmental beliefs and values not only of the public in each of our countries but also of various elites that might be active in that social change process. It seemed to us that environmental leaders would be likely to be a vanguard pointing out deficiencies in the relationship between man and nature within the current dominant belief structure; the environmental elite was to be selected randomly from the officers and leaders of environmental organizations. The English team believed that there were two distinct environmental elites in their country so they sampled from two environmental groups and treated them separately in their analysis. The business community is an important political force in these three advanced industrial countries that is likely to defend the belief that humans should dominate nature and extract wealth from it. We reasoned that we would most likely find a rearguard opposing the environmental vanguard within the business leadership structure; business leaders were to be sampled from national directories of major corporations. Since public officials have the responsibility to make authoritative decisions about the future direction of society, we believed it important to include a sample of them as part of the social change process we were investigating. In the United States, both elected and appointed officials from all three levels of government were sampled, while the team in England sampled appointed and elected officials in central and local government. The team in Germany sampled highly placed administrative officials in 1980 but in 1982 they sent the questionnaire to each member of the national parliament (Bundestag).

Labor leaders also constitute an important socio-political force and samples of them were drawn from national directories in England and the United States. In the United States, in the first wave, we also included a sample of media gatekeepers (defined as key persons within the print or broadcast media who decide which stories will go in the newspaper or appear on the air). This leadership group did not show very distinctive characteristics in the first wave study and, since we were short of funds for the second wave, they were dropped on the second wave.

Sampling procedures varied somewhat from country to country because of different traditions and possibilities. The United States team did not have sufficient funds to "rent" a national area probability sample such as those used by national polling organizations. Instead, they drew their own sample using the following procedure. The geographically contiguous 48 states and Hawaii were divided into eight regions and were stratified into urban, suburban, and rural areas. Once sampling points were identified by the stratification procedure, households were randomly sampled from recent telephone books for each of those areas.[1] A systematic procedure designed to provide equal numbers of males and females with a wide age distribution was used for selection of adult respondents within each of the households receiving a questionnaire. Ultimately, 53% of the public responded (see Table 1.1 p. 00 for response rates for all groups for each of the three countries).[2] This same public sample was used for the 1982 study. The first mailing in 1982 went to all identified households for which a questionnaire had not been returned as undeliverable. This mailing produced a good response from those who returned a questionnaire the last time but a very poor response from those who had not. The two subsequent mailings were confined to those who had returned last time, in 1980, in order to save funds; 53% of the households that returned the first time also returned a second time. (Details on sampling and fieldwork for the U.S. study are presented as an annex to this appendix.)

In the United Kingdom, the public sample was drawn, using a systematic random procedure, from all the electoral registers for England. This same procedure was used in 1982. The German team contracted the services of the Institut für Demoskopie Allensbach to distribute their questionnaire to a "two-step" stratified sample of the public used by that firm. The basis for this sample is a complete tally of all eligible voters for the Bundestag election of 1976. An updated sample by that firm based on the 1980 West German parliamentary elections was used in 1982.

As mentioned, two samples of environmentalists were drawn in England. One sample, called Nature Conservationists, were members of the Somerset Trust for Nature Conservation; the data show that this is a group of fairly conservative people who want to keep the present social structure and who also wish to conserve and protect nature. The other sample was drawn from a more reform-oriented group called the Conservation Society that appears to be similar in beliefs and values to the Friends of the Earth or the Sierra Club in the United States. For the 1982 survey, only members of the Conservation Society were sampled. Environmental respondents in the United States were drawn randomly from lists of board members and regular members supplied by the Sierra Club, the Nature Conservancy, Friends of the Earth, and the Environmental Defense Fund. Our analysis of first-wave data showed that this group was quite reform-oriented. We decided to supplement this sample in 1982 by systematically including more officers from organizations of the nature conservationist type; they were selected systematically from the *Conservation Directory*. This will enable us to distinguish nature conservationists from reform environmentalists and analyze their responses separately. It is important to remember that when the total environmentalist sample for 1982 is compared with 1980, the 1982 group will be more "conservative" on most dimensions.

The German team used a different procedure for selecting their environmentalist sample. In Germany, a special directory was published in 1979 titled, *Bürger im Umweltschutz*. This directory is a compilation of environmentally interested groups and organizations which had been active on behalf of environmental causes; 112 of these groups were selected at random from this directory. Each group was sent 4 copies of the questionnaire and was asked to distribute these among their members and have them filled out and returned. This procedure produced a rather low response rate (see Table 1.1). Using an updated version of the same directory in 1982, one copy of the questionnaire was sent to each of 575 citizen action groups with the same request. This time the response rate of 47% was much higher.

Business leaders were sampled from business directories in each country. In Germany, 400 persons were selected randomly from a directory titled *Leitende Männer der Wirtschaft*, published in 1979. In 1982, 500 persons were randomly selected from the 1981 version of that work which was then titled *Leitende Männer und Frauen der Wirtschaft*; 31% responded. In the United Kingdom, a sample of business leaders was drawn randomly from the *Directory of Directors*. In the United States, business leaders were sampled from two directories so as to include both large and small business in the sample. One hundred leaders of large corporations were randomly selected from the *Fortune 500* and 400 from Standard and Poor's *Corporations, Directors and Executives*. The questionnaire was them mailed either to the board chairman, the president, or one of the leading vice presidents. A supplementary sample was drawn from Standard and Poor's for the 1982 study.

The public officials samples also were drawn somewhat differently in each country. In the United States, approximately 90 federally elected officials and another 90 highly placed federally appointed officials were randomly selected from official directories. Similarly sized samples of elected and appointed state officials and local officials also were selected, mainly from the same areas in which we selected our sample of the public. The elected and appointed officials samples were analyzed separately for many of our analyses. For the 1982 study, we returned to as many of the appointed and elected officials as were still in office; no supplementary samples were drawn.

In the United Kingdom, the public officials were sampled from *Dodd's Parliamentary Companion*, which includes appointed and elected officials. In the German Federal Republic, the public officials were all holders of high administrative positions dealing with environmental policies. Each official identified in the sample was sent ten copies of the questionnaire, asked to fill in one himself, and distribute the others to people in his institution requesting them also to fill it out and return it to project headquarters. In 1982, the German team abandoned that procedure and sent questionnaires to all members of the German Bundestag; 21% responded.

Labor union respondents in the United States were drawn randomly from the latest issue of *Who's Who in Labor*. A supplementary sample was drawn from *The Encyclopedia of Associations* for the 1982 study. In England, the trade unionists were sampled from the *Trade Union Handbook*. No trade union sample was drawn in Britain in 1982. The German team did not include a sample of labor leaders.

In the United States, the media gatekeeper sample was randomly drawn from the *1978 Media Encyclopedia 29th Edition, Working Press of the Nation, Newspaper Directory*, and *Radio and TV Directory*. As an economy measure, no media sample was drawn for the 1982 study.

The response rates reported in Table 1.1 range from 82 down to about 20%, generally averaging near 50%. These response rates may be considered reasonably satisfactory for a mail questionnaire study. Although the response rates are lower than would normally be expected of a personal interview study, they are not drastically lower.[2] We have searched to see if systematic bias was introduced into our sample (see the annex) and have been unable to discover any significant bias. In studying the data, we have been struck again and again by similarities in response patterns within the public and also within various elites as we compare across countries. Comparisons from 1980 to 1982 also show many stable response patterns. The differences that we have uncovered make good theoretical sense, lending increased confidence in our results.

Samples provide a basis for two kinds of inferences. If the sample closely reflects the distribution of characteristics in a geographically defined population (such as the public in a state or nation), one can validly infer the distributions to be found in the population from the distributions found in the sample. This first kind of inference is used when statements such as "Seventy percent of the American people support the environmental movement" are made. Samples also give us a basis for estimating variance on specific dimensions; this is the second kind of inference. Typically, we look to see if two dimensions co-vary. We may report such a finding in a statement like, "There is a .54 correlation between the belief that humans are seriously damaging nature and the environmentalism scale." While both sets of inferences are based on random sampling, it is possible to have a good sample of variance even though a random sample is not a closely accurate representation of some geographically defined population. Keeping this distinction in mind, we can say that we have an excellent sample of variance on the issues we are studying but, perhaps, only a good sample of the geographical distribution of the characteristics we measured. All in all, we conclude that we can make reliable and valid inferences about relationships between variables and somewhat weaker inferences, but still useful, with respect to the frequency or incidence of characteristics within populations.

Questionnaire Design

The content of the questionnaire was worked out in two international conferences. A core element of the questionnaire was identical across the participating countries. In a given country, a research team could add additional questions suited to its special situation or to specially planned analyses (the questionnaire used in 1980 is found in Appendix A and the questionnaire used in 1982 is found in Appendix B; the items that were core for the three countries are coded with a C).

The questionnaire is divided into several parts. The first part is made up of agree-disagree items focusing on beliefs about environment and society, many of which were drawn from a scale developed by the British team and had been used in previous studies in England and the United States. Factor analysis discloses that these items cluster into belief structures with respect to the environment that are similar in all three countries.

In the second part of the questionnaire respondents were asked to choose between contrasting statements about emphases or directions their society should be taking. These questions were newly designed for this study to measure basic beliefs about societal functioning and the relationship of humans to nature.

The third section in 1980 dealt with environmentally related behavior. Analysis of the data from the 1980 study showed that these variables did not relate very strongly to other sections of the study and did not seem to be working as well as intended. The section was drastically reduced for the 1982 study.

The fourth section of the questionnaire dealt with the perceived urgency for public action on environmental problems as well as some related judgements with respect to the appropriateness of such action. A special component of that section dealt with the levels of trust people had in various societal institutions for solving environmental problems. The next section of the questionnaire incorporated a number of items that dealt in one way or another with environmentalism.

The next section of the questionnaire (numbers beginning with 5) incorporates mainly the items that were discretionary and unique to the U.S. study. The one exception was a set of items (5.8–5.14) in the 1982 questionnaire dealing with sources of information with respect to environmental problems; that was core in all three countries. In the 1980 questionnaire this section included the six items that had been used in the Louis Harris study against which we wished to compare our own data. Those items had not been repeated in Harris studies in recent times so could not be used for comparison in 1982; but we did include items 5.15 and 5.16 that had been used by Harris recently against which we could compare our own distributions.

The last section of the questionnaire incorporated typical demographic items. We tried hard, particularly in 1982, to make them comparable across countries so far as different cultural traditions permitted (the question on party preference had to be unique to each country, for example).

The questionnaire includes only a fraction of the topics we would have liked to cover; it had to be kept short so that people could fill it out in about 20 minutes. The simplistic way in which some issues had to be presented frustrated some sophisticated respondents who wanted to explain their views more fully. On the other hand, we are sure that some persons found the questionnaire too difficult and simply discarded it rather than try to fill it out; we show a poorer response rate for less educated people. The questionnaire deals with issues that mainly have meaning in advanced industrial societies. A colleague translated the questionnaire into Korean and tried to utilize it in a field study in South Korea. He reported that so many respondents found it impossible to comprehend the questions that he had to abandon the study. Another colleague is adopting a translated version of the questionnaire for a study using personal interviews in Taiwan. We are curious to know what his success will be there. It is our impression from the feedback we have received that many respondents found the questionnaire challenging and illuminating; they also seemed to feel that we were asking important questions. Given the length and difficulty of the questionnaire, we believe they must have felt very strongly motivated or else we could not have achieved the very satisfactory response rate that we realized.

NOTES

1. The New York Telephone Company estimates that 98.7% of dwellings in the U.S. have a telephone. Despite that impressive figure, such a sampling method is biased against low income Blacks and Hispanic minorities who clearly are underrepresented in our sample. This fact should be kept in mind when interpreting the data. We wish we had the funds for personal interviews; failing that, we must see what we can learn from the data we have.

2. The phone interview survey conducted by Research and Forecasts, Inc., for the Continental Group (1982) had an only slightly better 57% response rate from their public sample.

Annex to Appendix E

Sampling and Fieldwork Procedures
for the U.S. Study 1980 & 1982

Introduction

Drawing the samples for a mail questionnaire study of the general public in the United States and of five leadership groupings, constituted a sizable challenge. There is no single listing of all persons 18 years of age and older in the United States from which names could be selected for a public sample. Voter registration lists that are suitable for this purpose in some other countries are not suitable in the United States. Not only are they generally not available for this purpose, but, even more importantly, approximately ¼ of American adults do not register to vote.

Most nationwide survey organizations in the United States use a four-stage area probability sample to identify households and then use a standard procedure for selecting a respondent within the household for a specific interview. Such a sample is very expensive to develop and maintain, hence, the cost of "renting" such a sample from one of the survey organizations was far beyond the monetary resources available to us.

Since a high percentage of American households have telephones, (New York Telephone estimated for us that 98% of U.S. households have telephones), we thought of using telephone books to draw a random sample of households. A basic difficulty with that method is that a certain proportion of telephone subscribers (various estimates lie between 10 and 15 percent) have unlisted numbers and, therefore, the household telephone number does not appear in the phonebook. To get around that problem, some survey organizations use random digit dialing. With this method, each telephone number has an equal probability of entering the sample whether or not it is listed in the phonebook. This is a moderately expensive but reliable method for a local survey. If it is used nationwide, requiring long distance charges, it is prohibitively expensive.

Selecting the U.S. Public Sample

Consequently, out of necessity, we returned to the idea of selecting households from telephone directories. Some studies suggest that samples drawn from directories are not fundamentally different from those drawn by random digit dialing (Ellison, 1980). This strategy introduced

143

some modest but not disabling biases into our sample since some households cannot afford telephones and others are unlisted numbers. These biases will be discussed lated under "sampling results".

To help insure that our sample of the general public drawn from telephone books would be as representative as possible, we stratified on several criteria to maximize the variance that we anticipated existed in the general population. As a first step in this stratification, the continental United States and Hawaii were divided up into the following eight regions (for more detail, see Cornwell, 1980):

1) Rural New England
2) The industrial heartland
3) The Southeast
4) Agricultural Mid-West
5) Prairie States
6) The arid Southwest
7) The Mountain States
8) The Pacific Northwest and Hawaii

It was decided to exclude Alaska from this regionalization because it is so sparsely settled and would be difficult to obtain thorough coverage by telephone directory. In regionalizing, we did not adhere strictly to state lines. The major consideration in the distinctions between regions was the main way that the people of that region related to their natural environment, particularly to land and agricultural production. The history of the region, particularly its settlement by white immigrants, also was important. Known political leanings of the people in the region also were relevant. Any regionalization that might have been attempted would have been a judgemental call. The one used here was designed to maximize variance on the characteristics that we believed were most relevant to this study.

Within each region, a target number of respondents was established based on the proportion the population of that region constituted of the total U.S. population. Areas within a region were further broken down by differentiating central city, suburbs, villages, and rural areas; a target number of respondents was then established for each of those categories based on the proportion that each size of place constituted of the total population of that region. Each specific sampling point was chosen randomly from a list of all possible sampling points defined by the specified characteristics within each of the regions. Generally, this meant that a specific central city was selected, its suburbs, small cities nearby, and a few rural areas at some moderate distance from the central city. This sampling design is spelled out in more detail in Table E.1.

The New York Telephone Company then assisted us in obtaining telephone directories from the places selected by this random procedure. In a few instances, substitutions had to be made since we could not

TABLE E.1
Sampling Design

Region # and Urbanized Area	Number of Persons Sampled				
	Suburban	City	Village	Rural	Total
#1—Lawrence-Haverhill, Mass.-N.H.	25	25	75 15 pers. 5 places	75 15 pers. 5 places	
Nashua, N.H.	25	25			300
Utica-Rome, N.Y.	25	25			
	75	75			
#2—New York, N.Y.	40	40	100 10 pers. 10 places	100 10 pers. 10 places	
Chicago-N.W. Indiana	40	40			
Akron, Ohio	40	40			
Toledo, Ohio	40	40			
Syracuse, N.Y.	40	40			1000
South Bend, Ind.-Mich.	40	40			
Rockford, Ill.	40	40			
Atlantic City, N.J.	40	40			
Meriden, Conn.	40	40			
Stubenville-Weirton, Ohio-W. Virginia	40	40			
	400	400			
#3—Miami, Fla.	31	31	100 10 pers. 10 places	100 10 pers. 10 places	
Atlanta, Ga.	31	31			
Richmond, Va.	31	31			
Raleigh, N.C.	31	31			
Gadsen, Ala.	31	31			696
El Paso, Tx.	31	31			
Knoxville, Tenn.	31	31			
Jackson, Miss.	31	31			
	248	248			
#4—St. Louis, Mo.	35	35	75 15 pers. 5 places	75 15 pers. 5 places	
Davenport-Rock Island-Moline, Iowa—Ill.	35	35		500	
Rochester, Minn.	35	35			
Milwaukee, Wis.	35	35			
Cincinatti, Ohio	35	35			
	175	175			
#5—Oklahoma City, Okla.	25	25	75 15 pers. 5 places	75 15 pers. 5 places	
Tulsa, Okla.	25	25			300
Sioux Falls, S.D.	25	25			
	75	75			
#6—Los Angeles, Cal.	34	34	100 10 pers. 10 places	100 10 pers. 10 places	
Phoenix, Ariz.	34	34			
Albuquerque, N.M.	34	34			608
Modesto, Cal.	34	34			
Salinas-Monterey, Cal.	34	34			
Simi Valley, Cal.	34	34			
	204	204			

TABLE E.1—*(Continued)*
Sampling Design

Region # and Urbanized Area	Suburban	City	Number of Persons Sampled Village		Rural		Total
#7—Denver, Col.	25	25	75	15 pers. 5 places	75	15 pers. 5 places	300
Boise City, Idaho	25	25					
Ogden, Utah	25	25					
	75	75					
#8—Spokane, Wash.	25	25	75	15 pers. 5 places	75	15 pers. 5 places	300
Eugene, Oregon	25	25					
Honolulu, Hawaii	25	25					
	75	75					
Total Persons	1327	1327	675		675		4004

obtain telephone directories for a few of the places that were to be sampled. When an appropriate phone book had been acquired, careful procedures were followed for randomly selecting pages within the phone book and for selecting telephone subscribers from a given page. The names and addresses selected in this fashion were treated as a sample of households and were entered onto a computer tape so that multiple copies of the household sample list could be generated for mailing purposes. The total household sample drawn in this fashion was 3,835.

Once a household had been selected to receive a questionnaire, we still needed a system for randomization of age and sex distributions of possible respondents within households. We decided that ¼ of the letters we mailed would ask for the youngest male over 18 to fill out and return the questionnaire; another ¼ requested the oldest male to do so; another ¼ asked the youngest female over 18 to fill out and return the questionnaire; and the last ¼ of the letters requested the oldest female to do so. Four different cover letters were prepared and assigned in advance to the selected households.

This procedure for selecting respondents within households by sex and age produced a reasonably satisfactory distribution by sex; males were slightly overrepresented in our sample (see Table E.5). When we compare our sample with census estimates by age, we find some underrepresentation of young people. Since there is a slight tendency for younger persons and females to more likely favor environmental causes, this public sample, if it is biased at all, is likely to be a little less environmentally-oriented than the overall population of the U.S. To put the point another way, this sample conservatively estimates the environmentalism of the general population.

When we went back into the field in 1982, there were insufficient funds to draw a new public sample. Even though we realized that many people would have moved during the two-year interim, we did our best to obtain responses from as many of the same households as possible from the 1980 sample. Our first mailing in 1982 went to all of the households we had contacted in 1980 and to which we presumed a letter had been delivered. Those households that returned a questionnaire in 1980 also tended to respond at a favorable rate in 1982. Those that had not returned in 1980 responded at a very poor rate in 1982; in the interest of saving our scarce resources, the two subsequent "reminder" mailings were made only to households that had responded in 1980.

Selecting the Leadership Groups

In selecting our samples of leaders, we first compiled lists from various sources and then randomly selected respondents from those lists. In the case of environmentalists, lists of members and board members were supplied by the Sierra Club, the Nature Conservancy, Friends of the Earth, and the Environmental Defense Fund. Three hundred fifty-eight potential respondents were selected from those lists in 1980. In 1982, we went back to those same people, except for those whose questionnaires had been returned undeliverable, this included 107 who did not respond in 1980. In addition, we selected a supplementary sample of environmentalists from the *Conservation Directory*. In doing so, we deliberately incorporated a larger proportion of people who were officers of nature conservationist type organizations such as hunting and fishing clubs. These groups typically are less interested in basic social change; on many measures, the 1982 environmentalist sample is more "conservative" than the 1980 environmentalist sample.

A deliberate attempt was made to include both large and small businesses in the business leaders sample. Approximately 100 corporations were randomly selected from the *Fortune 500*. Approximately 400 additional corporations were selected from Standard and Poors, *Corporations, Directors, and Executives*. The letter requesting them to participate in this study generally was addressed either to the board chairman, the president, or a senior vice president. In 1982, questionnaires were sent only to those business leaders who had responded in 1980. A supplementary sample of 184 was drawn from Standard and Poors, approximately 50% of these responded.

On the public official sample, we targeted to select both elected and appointed officials from all three levels of government. When these two criteria were arrayed in a matrix, we selected approximately 90 names in each cell, to wit:

1) 90 members of the U.S. Congress were chosen randomly from an official list.
2) 90 highly placed appointed federal administrators were chosen randomly from 10 federal agencies.
3) 2 state senators and 1 assemblyman were randomly chosen from each of 32 state legislatures, the same states from which our general public sample was drawn.
4) In these same states, 3 appointed officials were selected who were most likely to be involved with environmental affairs; usually they were the commissioners of commerce, environment, and motor vehicles.
5) 90 local elected officials were selected from lists of local elected officials supplied by local Leagues of Women Voters or by local newspapers. The officials targeted for random selection were primarily mayors, city and town councilmen, and county legislators.
6) 90 local appointed officials were selected from lists obtained from the same sources that supplied the lists of local elected officials; persons sampled from this list consisted mainly of city managers, public works directors, and county administrators. Appointed officials responded at a much better rate (61%) than elected officials (30%). In 1982, we did not draw supplementary

samples of officials but mailed letters to all of the officials that had been sent the questionnaire in 1980 excluding only those whose questionnaires had been returned undeliverable or whom we knew to have left office (see Tables E.2 and E.3).

Labor union leaders were drawn randomly in 1980 from *Who's Who in Labor*. This directory had not been updated by 1982 and was now about 5 years old. A supplementary sample was drawn, instead, from the *Encyclopedia of Associations* for the 1982 study. The sample of media gatekeepers was used only in 1980 and was drawn randomly from lists derived from the following sources: *The 1978 Media Encyclopedia, 29th edition*, the *Working Press of the Nation*, the *Newspaper Directory*, and the *Radio and TV Directory*.

Fieldwork Procedures

Approximately 5,800 questionnaires were mailed out during the last two weeks of January 1980. About 20% of those questionnaires (1108) were returned by the postal service as undeliverable; nearly 26% of the general public sample drawn from the telephone books were returned undeliverable (see Table E.2). It was not possible to tell in many cases why the questionnaire was not delivered. A major factor is that some telephone books were a year or two old and many Americans (somewhere in the neighborhood of 20%) move in any given year. Some of the respondents listed in the telephone books had died. It also was apparent that a significant proportion of undeliverable questionnaires resulted from carelessness in the postal service and/or unwillingness by postal clerks to fill in a forwarding address. In several instances, for example, a filled in questionnaire would be returned by a respondent after we had already mailed a second questionnaire; yet, the second questionnaire would be returned as undeliverable. This large proportion of undelivered questionnaires effectively reduced the general public sample to 2,849. Since the leadership samples contained specific names and addresses, there was a small proportion of undeliverable questionnaires; but, even in these cases, there was some attrition due to failure to deliver. In 1982, six questionnaires addressed to sitting Members of Congress were returned undeliverable.

If a questionnaire was not returned after a lapse of approximately three weeks, a reminder card was sent. The first wave of reminder cards was mailed out in the period February 10–15, 1980. If the reminder card did not produce a completed questionnaire, a second was sent with the same cover letter as had been mailed previously. Most of this second mailing took place toward the end of February 1980. If a questionnaire was not returned after another lapse of approximately three weeks, a second reminder card was mailed during the third week of March 1980. We decided to see if a third mailing of the questionnaire could boost response rates. This time we included a very short cover

TABLE E.2
Sample Summary U.S. 1980.

	Public	Environ-mentalists	Business Leaders	Labor Leaders	Elected Officials	Appointed Officials	Media Gatekeepers	Total
Original Sample no. of Letters Mailed	3835	358	497	197	266	268	264	5,685
Returned Undeliverable	986	25	43	17	10	18	9	1,108
Presumed Delivered	2849	333	454	180	256	250	255	4,577
Returned Refused	164	3	17	4	12	8	4	212
Useable Responses	1513	225	223	85	78	153	105	2,382
Response Rate	53%	67.5%	49%	47%	30%	61%	41%	52%

letter that said simply that we really did mean it, we needed their response, and would very much appreciate it if they would fill in the questionnaire and return it. This mailing produced approximately 400 additional usable questionnaires and was well worth the effort. In 1982, we followed essentially the same procedures except that we did not use the two mailings of reminder cards (again to conserve resources).

Sampling Results and Confidence Levels

The thorough follow-up procedures just detailed produced a reasonably satisfactory return rate for a mail questionnaire study. Tables E.2 and E.3 provide detailed information on sample size, proportion of non-deliverable letters, response rates of final sample sizes for 1980 and 1982. Generally we found in 1980 that about 50% of the persons we approached returned a usable questionnaire (the rate for the general public was 53%). Over 60% of the environmentalists and appointed officials responded but only 30% of the elected officials did so. Not only are elected officials very busy people but many of them also have a policy of not responding to any questionnaires; this is particularly true of members of Congress.

The 1982 sample summary in Table E.3 is much more complicated. We wished to return to as many of the 1980 respondents as we could reach so that we could compare at an individual level their responses in 1982 with responses to the same items in 1980. We counted on some attrition and felt that we should draw supplementary samples where possible. The attrition turned out to be greater than we had anticipated. Our first mailing to the public in 1982 went to all of the households to which a questionnaire presumably had been delivered in 1980. Only a disappointingly small 5% of those households not responding in 1980 responded in 1982, but a much higher percentage responded from households that had returned in 1980. To conserve resources, we did not send anymore questionnaires in 1982 to non-responding households from 1980. In order to differentiate panel from non-panel respondents, we included a question at the very top of the questionnaire that asked respondents if they had filled out a similar questionnaire in 1980. We soon discovered that that was a poor screening question. Some respondents failed to check either response. Careful comparison of demographic factors such as sex and age disclosed that many others had a poor memory. We finally had to use five demographic characteristics to screen every case so as to be able to reliably assign people to the panel. If there was any doubt whether this was indeed the same person, the respondent was assigned to the non-panel category. Using these tight criteria, only 27% of the public sample (332 persons) could reliably be judged as the same person who responded in 1980. Our 1982 letter requested someone else at that address to fill out the questionnaire if the person who did it in 1980 was not available; 312

Table E.3
Sample Summary U.S. 1982

	Public	Environ-mentalists	Business Leaders	Labor Leaders	Appointed Officials	Elected Officials
1980 Sample Frame Used in 1982						
Letters Mailed	1513[a]	332[b]	219[c]	84[d]	244[e]	232[f]
Non-Deliverable	301	59	31	8	30	10
Presumed Delivered	1212	273	188	76	214	222
Panel-Useable Responses	332	112	106	28	76	45
Response Rate	27%	41%	56%	37%	36%	20%
1982 Supplementary Sample						
Letters Mailed	1249[g]	223	184	214	none	none
Non-Deliverable	212	17	30	7		
Presumed Delivered	1037	206	154	207		
New Respondents Useable Responses	51	124	77	86		
Response Rate	5%	60%	50%	42%		
Returned by someone else at 1980 R's address	312	38	19	16	39	3
Total Non-Panel	363	162	96	102	39	3
Grand Total	695	274	202	130	115	48
Overall Response Rate	53%	57%	59%	46%	54%	22%

a–3 mailings to 1980 respondents
b–Sent to respondents and non-respondents in 1980 sample.
c–Sent only to those who responded in 1980.
d–Sent only to those who responded in 1980.
e–Sent to respondents and non-respondents in 1980 sample.
f–Sent to respondents and non-respondents in 1980 sample.
g–1 mailing to 1980 non-respondents

persons did so. Interestingly, the overall response rate to the public mailing was 53% in 1982, the same percentage as in 1980.

The 1982 questionnaire was mailed to all of the 1980 environmentalist sample, respondents and non-respondents alike. This is apparently quite a mobile group as they were difficult to track down; we could only assign 41% of them to the panel. There was a fairly good 60% response rate from the supplementary sample and an additional 38 questionnaires came in from someone else at the same address as 1980 respondents.

Business leaders seem to be more "settled in" so we managed to get 56% of the 1980 respondents in our panel; the supplementary sample also responded at a 50% rate.

The sample of labor leaders, that was already small from 1980, suffered further attrition in 1982 with only 37% clearly assignable as panel. An additional 86 respondents were gained from a supplementary sample producing an overall labor leaders sample of 130 with an overall response rate of 46%.

No supplementary sample of public officials was drawn in 1982 but questionnaires were mailed to the entire public official list from 1980, except where a questionnaire had been returned undeliverable or where we knew the officials had left office. In any case, as with the other leadership groups, the letter had been addressed to a specific person and we requested that person only to respond. Despite that request, we still found a significant percentage of returned questionnaires that we could not match up demographically to be certain they were the same respondent; they were assigned to the non-panel group. It can be seen in Table E.3 that appointed officials were much better about responding than elected officials.

How much confidence do we have that our respondents are a reasonably accurate sample of the universe from which they are drawn? Among leadership groups, we are most confident of the environmentalists and business leaders samples. We have had sufficient experience with both waves of the data to feel fairly confident that the considerable difference we find between these two groups reflects a real difference in their respective populations. As detailed above, the public officials were a complex group to define. The response rates were so different between appointed and elected officials that we felt that it made more sense to treat them somewhat separately. Both groups cover such a wide spectrum, however, that we expected that their beliefs and values probably would not differ very much from that of the public; later analysis showed that to be true. The labor leaders sample was comparatively small in 1980, but the return rate was reasonably satisfactory. The supplementary sample strengthened it in 1982 and it can be taken in that year as a reasonable approximation of thinking among labor leaders. The return rate for media gatekeepers in 1980 was somewhat lower, and the sample size was not as large as for business leaders and environmentalists; given that, projections from this sample to the total universe of media gatekeepers should be made cautiously. The reader will recall that no sample of media gatekeepers was drawn in 1982.

We have two basic criteria for judging the representativeness of the general public sample. First, it was explained earlier that we included six items in our questionnaire that were identical to items that Louis Harris Associates included in an exceptionally large personal interview survey conducted in November 1979 with 7,010 respondents nationwide. By comparing response curves from those six items, for their sample and for ours, we can estimate whether or not the lower response rate to a mail questionnaire introduced a systematic bias compared to that of the larger personal interview study. Figures E.1–E.6 graphically compare the response curves from our sample to that of the Harris sample on those six questions. Note that the curves generally are very similar and that no consistent bias can be discerned. Careful study also discloses that the Harris curves typically have a W shape whereas the curves from our sample are smoother. We believe that this difference stems from the way that the items were introduced. Our phraseology read:

> The following are some opposite opinions about the direction in which this country *should be* moving today. Please *circle a numbered box* on the scale indicating how strongly you prefer one direction or the other for our country.

The introduction to these items on the Harris survey read:

> This card lists some opposite opinions about the direction in which this country *should be* moving today. For each pair of statements, tell me the letter and number that best represents where you stand. For example, if you feel *very strongly* that our country should emphasize spending on space, military, and defense programs, you should mark "a-3" on the *left* side of the card; if you feel *very strongly* that our country should emphasize spending on housing, health, and social programs, you should pick "b-3" on the *right* side of the card. If you are neutral or have no strong feelings either way, you should pick the middle choice, that is, "O" (ZERO). *You can pick any letter and number* to show in which direction and just how strongly you feel this country should be moving today.

Note that the Harris phraseology invited the respondent to think first about one extreme and then about the other extreme, and then the middle; this may have produced the "W" pattern that can be observed in their curves. A certain proportion of the people did in fact take one extreme or the other or the middle as the introductory statement invited them to do. Had those curves been smoothed out, they would have been strikingly close to the curves shown for our sample. We cannot conclude with full confidence that our sampling and fieldwork

Figure E.1

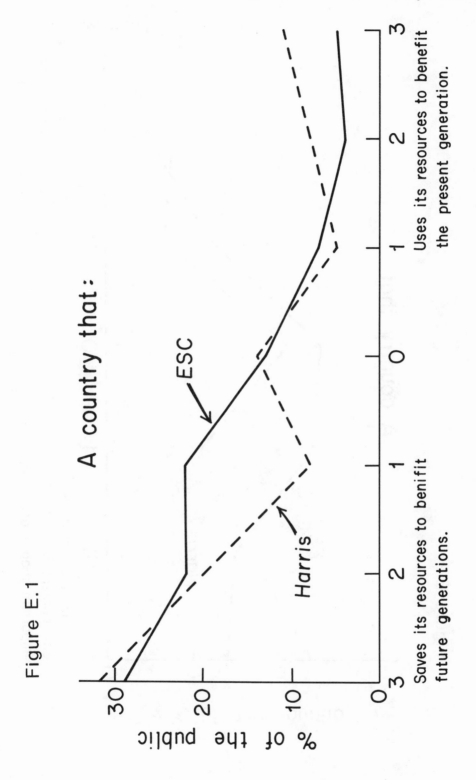

Figure E.2

A country that:

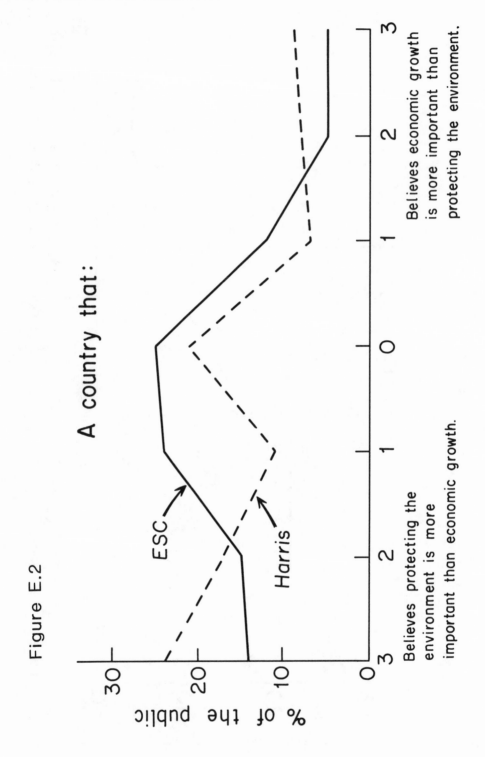

% of the public

Believes protecting the
environment is more
important than economic growth.

Believes economic growth
is more important than
protecting the environment.

ESC

Harris

Figure E.3

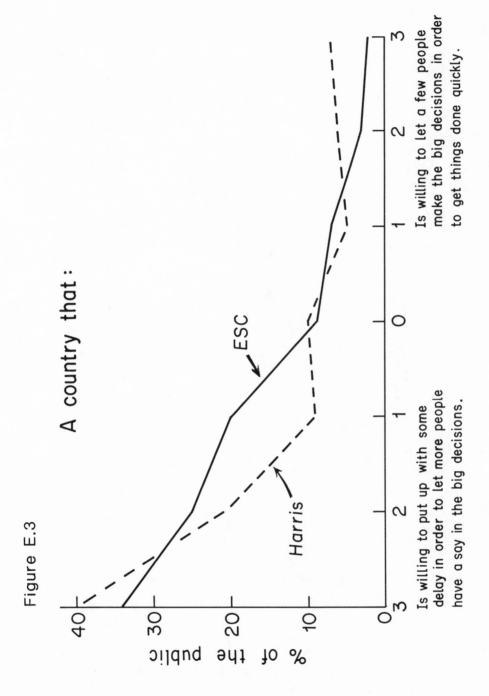

A country that :

% of the public

ESC

Harris

Is willing to put up with some delay in order to let more people have a say in the big decisions.

Is willing to let a few people make the big decisions in order to get things done quickly.

Figure E.4

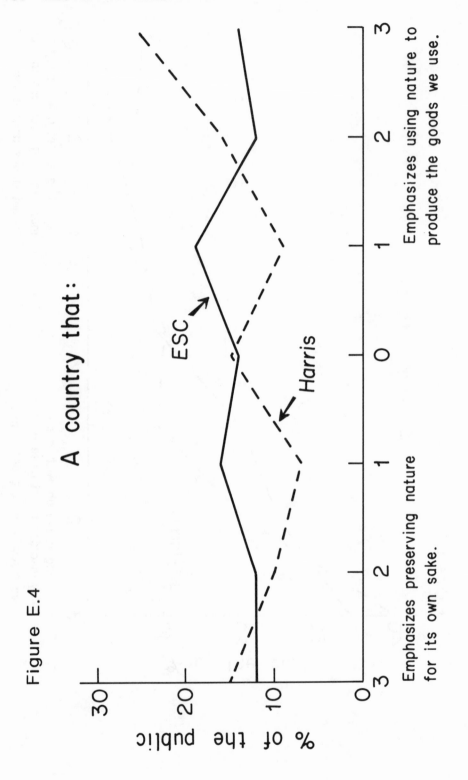

A country that:

Figure E.5

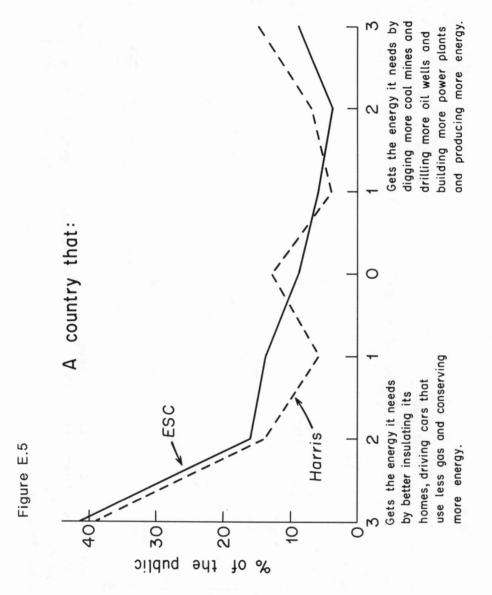

Figure E.6

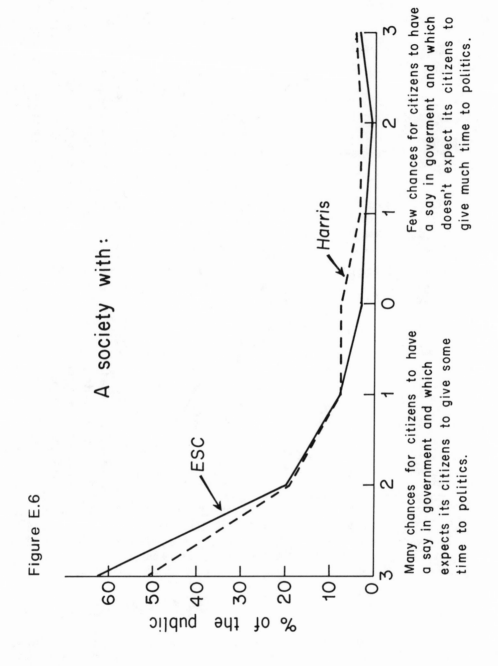

A society with:

% of the public

Many chances for citizens to have a say in government and which expects its citizens to give some time to politics.

Few chances for citizens to have a say in goverment and which doesn't expect its citizens to give much time to politics.

procedures did not introduce biases on other questions, but for these items we are unable to discern any systematic bias. Since a bias did not show up here, it is unlikely that it is present in other items either.

When we repeated our study in 1982, we contacted the Harris organization to see if it might be possible to use a similar procedure to see whether our 1982 sampling methodology introduced any systematic bias. Unfortunately, the Harris organization had not repeated any of these items in more recent studies. We did include two items on the 1982 questionnaire that had been used in the fall of 1981 by the Harris organization; those response patterns are compared in Table E.4. The Harris survey was conducted using personal interviews; the "not sure" category was not offered to the respondents but it was coded if it was volunteered. We felt compelled to include it as a possible response on the written questionnaire. Its presence before them apparently invited many respondents to take the "not sure" category on the written questionnaire. Since these questions involved fairly complicated tradeoffs, a fairly high percentage of "not sures" may well be more reflective of people's true feelings than those elicited in the personal interview situation. If the proportions taking the remaining content categories are compared, it seems that our 1982 public sample is slightly less pro-environment than the Harris sample. This "conservative" bias should be kept in mind when interpreting 1982 U.S. public responses reported in this book.

Another basis for judging the representativeness of the public sample is to compare demographic breakdowns in our sample with known breakdowns from the U.S. census estimates. Those comparisons are made in Table E.5. As can be seen in that Table, our 54% return from males in 1980 is slightly higher than the percentage of males in the adult population (this differential was reduced somewhat in the 1982 sample); this may result from the cultural bias that generally lists the male head of the family in phone books.

The 1980 sample had fewer young people than was estimated by the census and somewhat more in the older categories. By 1982, this difference was even more pronounced. That also helps to explain why a larger proportion of our sample reported being married and fewer reported being never married. These differences are partially traceable to telephone book sampling in that many young, unmarried persons may be in school or college; young people also are more likely to be mobile, hence not so likely to be listed in phone books. Because they are so mobile, it was more difficult to contact them again for the 1982 study which shows even greater attrition in the young, unmarried categories.

Our sample is also somewhat above the average in education and income. There probably are two reasons for this upward bias:

1) Persons living in institutions, serving in the armed forces, or being away from home in college (who also would tend to have

TABLE E.4

Comparison of U.S. Public Response Patterns to Identical Items used in Harris Survey in 1981 and in ESC Survey Winter-Spring 1982

Item

"Congress is reconsidering the Clean Air Act, which is now ten years old. Given the costs involved in cleaning up the environment, do you think Congress should make the Clean Air Act stricter than it is now, keep it about the same, or make it less strict?"

| | (Percentage saying) Harris | | |
	5/81	9/81	ESC
Make it stricter	38	29	35
Keep about the same	48	51	38
Make it less strict	12	17	8
Not sure	2	3	18.5

"The Clean Air Act does not permit the consideration of costs when setting standards for the protection of human health. The Reagan Administration is considering asking Congress to require that pollution standards designed to protect human health be relaxed if the costs are too high. Do you favor or oppose relaxing pollution standards affecting human health if the costs are too high?"

| | (Percentage saying) Harris | |
	9/81	ESC
Favor relaxing standards	32	52
Oppose relaxing standards	65	52
Not sure	3	27.5

TABLE E.5
Comparison of Public Sample Characteristics with U.S. Census Estimates of Population
Characteristics

	1980 Census* (unless otherwise noted) %		Environmental Survey Sample	
			1980	1982
Sex				
males 20 & over	47.4		54	52
female 20 & over	52.6		46	48
Marital Status—adults 18 & older				
never married	20		12	10
married	65		73	75
widowed	7		8	7.5
divorced or separated	6		6	5.5
Age				
15–19	12	18–20	4	3
20–29	23	21–30	19	15
30–39	18	31–40	20	19
40–49	13	41–50	17	16
50–59	13	51–60	19	22
60–64	6	61–70	13	16
65+	15	71+	9	9
Education				
0–8	17.5		7	6
9–11	13.9		10	9
H.S. Grad.	36.8		30	31
13–15	14.8		27	27
Finished College	17		13	12
		17+yrs.	13	15
Family Income (1979 est.)				
less than $5,000	7		6	5
5,000–9,999	13.6		11	9
10,000–14,999	15.6		15	12
15,000–19,999	15		15	11
20,000–24,000	14.4		18	14
25,000–34,999	19.2		18	25.5
35,000+	15.5		14	25
Race				
White	83.2		92	94
Black	11.7		2	2
Other	4		6	4

*Source: *The Statistical Abstract of the United States, 1981*

lower income and education) would not be sampled by our procedure.

2) Our questionnaire appears to have been fairly demanding for someone with poor intellectual capability; such persons were disproportionately likely to discard the questionnaire.

Another deficiency of our sample is that only 2% of our respondents are Black as compared to the 1977 census estimate that 10.4% of Americans are Black. Careful followers of public affairs probably recognize that few Blacks are active in environmental causes; that may account somewhat for their lower return rate. Additionally, Blacks tend to be of lower education and income than Whites and we have just seen that those of lower education and income are less likely to return the questionnaire.

The reader must judge for himself the extent to which these small demographic biases in our sample are likely to bias responses to our belief and value questions. In thinking about this, the reader should keep the following in mind:

1) Many studies have shown only slight relationships between demographic variables and environmental beliefs and values.

2) Age is the demographic variable most consistently related to environmentalism with young people being more environmentally oriented than older people. Since our sample is biased toward older people, it probably conservatively estimates the extent of environmentalism in the population.

3) This conservative bias may be offset by a tendency for people interested in the environment to more likely return the questionnaire than those disinterested in the environment.

4) Environmentalism is a bit more prominent in people of higher education but is a bit less prominent in people of higher income. Since income and education are positively correlated, these two biases probably are offsetting.

5) The persons represented in our sample seem to be more well established with stable positions in their communities than is true of the full range of the population. Established people who are well integrated into the community tend to be more active politically and to have more influence in public affairs. In other words, the people excluded from our sample are unlikely to have much impact on the course of public affairs. Since we are interested in linking environmental beliefs and values to social change and public policy, our sample is quite serviceable.

6) We compared responses to some of our belief and value items to responses to identical items used by national polling organizations with personal interviews. We found no consistent bias; their findings were essentially the same as ours.

7) An experienced survey research analyst who has worked with a data set for a long time develops a "feel" for the data. If the data fall into theoretically expected patterns, if it shows consistency across items and across time, if the correlations are reasonably strong and the significance tests report differences far beyond what could occur by one chance in a thousand, one develops a sense of confidence that the data are meaningful and informative. Having gone through that experience, I can report that the data "feel right" and are genuinely useful for understanding the phenomena we are studying.

REFERENCES

Agger, B. *Western Marxism: An Introduction.* Santa Monica: Goodyear, 1979.

Althoff, P., and Greig, W.H. "Environmental Pollution Control: Two Views From the General Population." *Environment and Behavior,* 1977, *9,* 441–56.

Anderson, R.W., and Lipsey, M.A. "Energy Conservation and Attitudes Toward Technology." *Public Opinion Quarterly,* 1978, *42* (1), 17–30.

Andrews, R.N.L. "Class Politics or Democratic Reform: Environmentalism and American Political Institutions." *Natural Resources Journal,* 1980, *20,* 221–241.

Arbuthnot, J., and Lingg, S. "A Comparison of French and American Environmental Behaviors, Knowledge and Attitudes." *International Journal of Psychology,* 1975, *10,* 275–81.

Banks, J.A. *The Sociology of Social Movements.* London: Macmillan, 1972.

Barnett, L.D. "A Study of the Relationship Between Attitudes Towards World Population Growth and U.S.A. Population Growth." *Journal of Bio-social Science,* 1973, *5,* 61–69.

Barnett, L.D. "Zero Population Growth, Inc.: A Second Study." *Journal of Bio-social Science,* 1974, *6,* January, 1–22.

Bartell, T. "Political Orientations and Public Response to the Energy Crisis." *Social Science Quarterly,* 1976, *57* (2), 430–436.

Bartell, T., and St. George, A. "A Trend Analysis of Environmentalists' Organizational Commitment, Tactic Advocacy, and Perceptions of Government." *Journal of Voluntary Action Research,* 1974, *3,* July-October, 41–46.

Benedict, R., Bone, H., Leavel, W. and Rice, R. "The Voters' Attitudes Toward Nuclear Power: A Comparative Study of Nuclear Moratorium Initiatives." *The Western Political Quarterly,* 1980, *33* (1), March, 7–23.

Borden, R.J., and Francis, J.L. "Who Cares About Ecology?: Personality and Sex Differences in Environmental Concern." *Journal of Personality,* 1978, *46,* 196–203.

Borklin, W. "The 'Greens' and the 'New Politics,' Goodbye to the Three Party System." Florence, Italy: European University Institute, 1981.

Boulding, K. *Ecodynamics: A New Theory of Societal Evolution.* Beverly Hills: Sage Publishers, 1978.

Bowman, F.H. "Public Opinion and the Environment: Post-Earth Day Attitudes Among College Students." *Environment and Behavior,* 1977, *9,* 385–416.

Buttel, F.H. "Age and Environmental Concern: A Multivariate Analysis." *Youth and Society,* 1979, *10* (3), 237–256.

167

Buttel, F.H. and Flinn, W.L. "The Structure of Support for the Environmental Movement, 1968–70." *Rural Sociology*, 1974, *39*, 56–69.

Buttel, F.H. and Flinn, W.L. "Environmental Politics: The Structuring of Partisan and Ideological Cleavages in Mass Environmental Attitudes." *Sociological Quarterly*, 1976a, *17*, 477–490.

Buttel, F.H. and Flinn, W.L. "Economic Growth vs. The Environment: Survey Evidence." *Social Science Quarterly*, 1976b, *57* (2), September, 410–420.

Buttel, F.H. and Flinn, W.L. "Conceptions of Rural Life and Environmental Concern." *Rural Sociology*, 1977, *42* (4), Winter, 544–555.

Buttel, F.H. and Flinn, W.L. "The Politics of Environmental Concern: The Impacts of Party Identification and Political Ideology on Environmental Attitudes." *Environment and Behavior*, 1978a, *10*, 17–36.

Buttel, F.H. and Flinn, W.L. "Social Class and Mass Environmental Beliefs: A Reconsideration." *Environment and Behavior*, 1978b, *10*, 433–450.

Buttel, F.H. and Johnson, D.E. "Dimensions of Environmental Concern: Factor Structure, Correlates, and Implications for Research." *The Journal of Environmental Education*, 1977, *9* (2), 49–64.

Buttel, F.H. and Larson, O.W., III. "Whither Environmentalism? The Future Political Path of the Environmental Movement." *Natural Resources Journal*, 1980, *20*, 323–344.

Catton, W.R., Jr. *Overshoot: The Ecological Basis of Revolutionary Change*. Urbana: University of Illinois Press, 1980.

Catton, W.R., Jr. and Dunlap, R.E. "Environmental Sociology: A New Paradigm." *American Sociologist*, 1978, *13*, 41–49.

Catton, W.R., Jr. and Dunlap, R.E. "A New Ecological Paradigm for Post-Exuberant Sociology." In special issue of *The American Behavioral Scientist*, 1980, *24*, 15–47, edited by R.E. Dunlap on "Ecology and the Social Sciences: An Emerging Paradigm."

Constantini, E. and Hanf, K. "Environmental Concern and Lake Tahoe: A Study of Elite Perceptions, Backgrounds and Attitudes." *Environment and Behavior*, 1972, *4* (2), 209–242.

Continental Group Report. *Toward Responsible Growth: Economic and Environmental Concern in the Balance*. Stamford, Connecticut, 1982.

Cornwell, M. "Sampling Procedures Used in the U.S. Component of an International Comparative Study of Environmental Beliefs and Values," (mimeo) Environmental Studies Center, SUNY/Buffalo, 1980.

Cotgrove, S.F. *Catastrophe or Cornucopia: The Environment, Politics and the Future*. Chichester/New York: Wiley and Sons, 1982.

Cotgrove, S.F. and Duff, A. "Environmentalism, Middle Class Radicalism and Politics." *Sociological Review*, 1980, *28* (2), 333–351.

Cotgrove, S.F. and Duff, A. "Environmental Values and Social Change." *British Journal of Sociology*, 1981, *32* (1), 92–110.

Cutler, S.C. "Community Concern for Pollution." *Environment and Behavior*, 1981, *13* (1), 105–124.

Devall, W.B. "Conservation: An Upper-Middle Class Social Movement, A Replication." *Journal of Leisure Research*, 1970a, *2* (Spring), 123–126.

Devall, W.B. "The Governing of a Voluntary Organization: Oligarchy and Democracy in the Sierra Club." Unpublished doctoral dissertation, Department of Sociology, University of Oregon, 1970b.

Devall, W.B. "The Deep Ecology Movement." *Natural Resources Journal*, 1980, *20*, 299–322.

Devall, W.B. "John Muir as Deep Ecologist." *Environmental Review*, 1982 (Spring).

Dillman, D.A. and Christenson, J.A. "The Public Value for Pollution Control." In W.R. Burch, Jr., N.H. Cheek, Jr. and L. Taylor (Eds.) *Social Behavior, Natural Resources, and the Environment.* New York: Harper and Row, 1972.

Dillman, D.A. and Christenson, J.A. "The Public Value for Air Pollution Control: A Needed Change of Emphasis in Opinion Structures." *Cornell Journal of Social Relations*, 1975, *10* (1), 73–95.

Duclos, P. "Unemployment or Pollution? Attitudes of the French Working Class to Environmental Issues." *International Journal of Urban and Regional Research*, 1981, *5* (1), 45–65.

Duff, A.G. and Cotgrove, S.F. "Social Values and the Choice of Careers in Industry." *Journal of Occupational Psychology*, 1982, *55*, 97–107.

Duncan, O.D., "From Social System to Ecosystem." *Sociological Inquiry* 1961, *31*, 140–149.

Dunlap, R.E. (Ed.). "Ecology and the Social Sciences: An Emerging Paradigm." In special issue of *The American Behavioral Scientist*, 1980, *24* (1).

Dunlap, R.E. and Dillman, D.A. "Decline in Public Support for Environmental Protection: Evidence From a 1970–74 Panel Study." *Rural Sociology*, 1976, *41*, 382–390.

Dunlap, R.E., Grieneeks, J.K. and Rokeach, M. "Human Values and Pro-Environmental Behavior." In W.D. Conn (Ed.) *Energy and Material Resources: Attitudes, Values, and Public Policy.* Boulder, CO: Westview Press, 1983.

Dunlap, R.E. and Van Liere, K. "Further Evidence of Declining Public Concern with Environmental Problems: A Research Note." *Western Sociological Review*, 1977, *8*, 108–112.

Dunlap, R.E. and Van Liere, K. "The New Environmental Paradigm." *The Journal of Environmental Education*, 1978, *9* (4), 10–19.

Ehrlich, P., and Ehrlich, A. *Extinction: The Causes and Consequences of the Disappearance of Species.* New York: Ballantine Books, 1981.

Ellison, Peter C. "Phone Directory Samples Just as Balanced as Samples from Computer Random Digit Dialing" *Marketing News*, 1980 13:8

Erskine, H. "The Polls: Pollution and Its Costs." *Public Opinion Quarterly*, 1972a, *36*, 120–135.

Erskine, H. "The Polls: Pollution and Industry." *Public Opinion Quarterly,* 1972b, *36* (Summer), 263–280.

Faich, R.G. and Gale, R.P. "The Environmental Movement From Recreation to Politics." *Pacific Sociological Review,* 1971, *14* (3), 270–287.

Feist, U., and Liepelt, K. "New Elites in Old Parties: Observations on a Side-Effect of the German Educational Reform." Paper presented at the XII World Congress of the International Political Science Association, Rio de Janeiro, August, 1982.

Fox, S. *John Muir and His Legacy: The American Conservation Movement.* Boston, Little Brown, 1981.

Harry, J., Gale, R. and Hendee, J. "Conservation: An Upper Middle Class Social Movement." *Journal of Leisure Research,* 1969, *1,* 246–254.

Hays, S.P. *Conservation and the Gospel of Efficiency.* Cambridge, MA: Harvard University Press, 1959.

Heberlein, T.A. "Norm Activation in Environmental Action." *Journal of Social Issues,* 1977, *33,* 207–211.

Hershey, M.R. and Hill, P.B. "Is Pollution a White Thing? Racial Differences in Pre-Adults' Attitudes." *The Public Opinion Quarterly,* 1977–1978, *41* (4), 439–458.

Honnold, J. "Predictors of Public Environmental Concern in the 1970's." In D. Mann (Ed.) *Environmental Policy Formation.* Lexington, MA: D.C. Heath Company, 1981, 63–75.

Honnold, J. and Nelson, L.D. "Age and Environmental Concern: Some Specification of Effects." Paper presented at the Annual Meeting of the American Sociological Association, Toronto, 1981.

Horvat, R.E. and Voelker, A.M. "Using A Likert Scale to Measure 'Environmental Responsibility'." *The Journal of Environmental Education,* 1976, *8* (1), 36–47.

Humphrey, C.R., and Buttel, F.R. *Environment, Energy and Society.* Belmont, Ca., Wadsworth, 1982.

Inglehart, R. "The Silent Revolution in Europe: Intergenerational Change in Post-Industrial Societies." *American Political Science Review,* 1971, *65,* 991–1017.

Inglehart, R. *The Silent Revolution: Changing Values and Political Styles Among Western Publics.* Princeton, New Jersey: Princeton University Press, 1977.

Inglehart, R. "Post-Materialism in an Environment of Insecurity." *American Political Science Review,* 1981, *75* (4), 880–900.

Inglehart, R. "Value Change in Japan and the West." *Comparative Political Studies,* 1982.

Jackson, E.L. "Perceptions of Energy Problems and the Adoption of Conservation Practices in Edmonton and Calgary." *The Canadian Geographer,* 1980, *24* (2), 114–130.

Kefalas, A., Sterios, G. and Carroll, A.B. "Perspectives on Environmental Protection: A Survey of the Executive Viewpoint." *Journal of Environmental Systems,* 1977, *6,* 229–242.

Kemp, J. *An American Renaissance: A Strategy for the 1980's.* New York: Harper & Row, 1979.

Koenig, D.J. "Additional Research on Environmental Activism." *Environment and Behavior,* 1975, *7,* 472–485.

Kohl, D.H. "The Environmental Movement: What Might It Be?" *Natural Resources Journal,* 1975 *15,* (April), 327–351.

Kreger, J. "Ecology and Black Student Opinion." *The Journal of Environmental Education.* 1973, *4* (3), 30–34.

Kromm, D.E., Probald, E. and Wall, G. "An International Comparison of Response to Air Pollution." *Journal of Environmental Management,* 1973, *1,* 363–375.

Kuhn, T.S. *The Structure of Scientific Revolutions.* Chicago, Illinois: University of Chicago Press, 2nd edition 1970 (1962).

Leiss, W. *The Domination of Nature.* Boston: Beacon Press, 1972.

Levine, A.G. *Love Canal: Science, Politics and People.* Lexington, MA: D.C. Heath, 1982.

Lovins, A. "Energy Strategy: The Road Not Taken?" *Foreign Affairs,* 1976 (Fall), 65–96.

Lovins, A. *Soft Energy Paths: Toward a Durable Peace.* New York: Harper Colophon Books, 1977.

Lowe, P.D. "Environmental Groups and Government in Britain." In P. Knoepfel and N. Watts (Eds.) *Environmental Politics and Policies.* Frankfurt/New York: Campus Verlag, 1982.

McConnell, G. "The Conservation Movement: Past and Present." *Western Political Quarterly,* 1954, *7,* 463–478.

McConnell, G. "The Environmental Movement: Ambiguities and Meanings." *Natural Resources Journal,* 1971, *11* (July).

McStay, J. and Dunlap, R. "Male-Female Differences in Concern for Environmental Quality: A Research Note." Scientific paper, Agricultural Research Center, Washington State University, Pullman, Washington, 1982.

McTeer, J.H. "Teenage-Adult Differences in Concern for Environmental Problems." *Journal of Environmental Education,* 1978, *9* (2), 20–23.

Mann, D.E. (Ed.). *Environmental Policy Formation: The Impact of Values, Ideology, and Standards.* Lexington, MA: D.C. Heath, 1981.

Marien, M. "The Two Post-Industrialisms and Higher Education." *World Future Society Bulletin,* 1982, (May/June) 13–28.

Mazmanian, D. and Sabatier, P. "Liberalism, Environmentalism, and Partisanship in Public Policy Making: The California Coastal Commissions." *Environment and Behavior,* 1981, *13* (3), 361–384.

Merchant, C. *The Death of Nature: Women, Ecology, and the Scientific Revolution.* San Francisco: Harper and Row, 1980.

Milbrath, L.W. "Environmental Beliefs: A Tale of Two Counties." Mimeo, Environmental Studies Center, State University of New York at Buffalo, 1975.

Milbrath, L.W. "Values and Beliefs that Distinguish Environmentalists From Non-Environmentalists." Paper delivered at the Annual Meeting of the International Society for Political Psychology, Washington, D.C., May 24–26, 1979.

Milbrath, L.W. "Using Environmental Beliefs and Values to Predict Tradeoffs and Choices Among Water Quality Plan Alternatives." *Socio-Economic Planning Sciences,* 1980, *14,* 129–136.

Milbrath, L.W. "Environmental Values and Beliefs of the General Public and Leaders in the United States, England and Germany." In D. Mann (Ed.) *Environmental Policy Formation: The Impact of Values, Ideology and Standards.* Lexington, MA: D.C. Heath, 1981a, 43–61.

Milbrath, L.W. "General Report: U.S. Component of a Comparative Study of Environmental Beliefs and Values." Mimeo, Occasional Paper Series, Environmental Studies Center, State University of New York at Buffalo, 1981b.

Milbrath, L.W. "The Relationship of Environmental Beliefs and Values to Politics and Government." Paper presented at the 4th Annual Conference of the International Society for Political Psychology, Mannheim, Germany, 1981c.

Milbrath, L.W. "Beliefs About Our Social Paradigm: Are We Moving to a New Paradigm? " Paper delivered at the 22nd Annual Convention of the International Studies Association, Philadelphia, March 18–21, 1981d.

Milbrath, L.W., and Goel, M.L. *Political Participation.* Washington, D.C.: University Press of America, 1982.

Milbrath, L.W. and Inscho, F. "The Environmental Problem as a Political Problem: An Agenda of Environmental Concerns for Political Scientists." In L. Milbrath and F. Inscho (Eds.) *The Politics of Environmental Policy.* Beverly Hills: Sage Publications, 1975, 7–34.

Miles, R.E. Jr. "The Origin and Meaning of Miles Law." *Public Administration Review,* 1978 (Sept.-Oct.) 399–403.

Mitchell, R.C. "The Public Speaks Again: A New Environmental Survey." *Resources,* 1978, *60.*

Mitchell, R.C. "Silent Spring/Solid Majorities." *Public Opinion,* 1979a, *2,* 16–20, 55.

Mitchell, R.C. "Since Silent Spring: Science, Technology and the Environmental Movement in the United States." In Norwegian Research Council, Institute for Studies in Higher Education, Report #1979:5. *Scientific Expertise and the Public Conference Proceedings,* 1979b.

Mitchell, R.C. "How 'Soft', 'Deep', or 'Left?' Present Constituencies in the Environmental Movement for Certain World Views." *Natural Resources Journal,* 1980a, *20,* 345–358.

Mitchell, R.C. *Public Opinion on Environmental Issues: Results of a National Survey.* Report for the Council on Environmental Quality. Washington, D.C.: United States Government Printing Office, 0–329–221/6586, 1980b.

Mitchell, R.C. "Polling on Nuclear Power: A Critique of the Polls After Three Mile Island." In A. Cantril (Ed.) *Polling on the Issues.* Washington, D.C.: Seven Locks Press, 1980c.

Mitchell, R.C. "From Elite Quarrel to Mass Movement." *Transaction/Society*, 1981, *18* (5), 76–84.

Mitchell, R.C. "Rationality and Irrationality in the Public's Perception of Nuclear Power." Paper presented at the 148th Annual Meeting of the American Association for the Advancement of Science, Washington, D.C., 1982.

Mitchell, R.C. "Public Opinion and Environmental Politics in the 1970s and 1980s" in Vig. and M.E. Kraft (Eds.) *Environmental Policy in the 1980s: Reagan's New Agenda*, Wash. D.C., Congressional Quarterly Press, 1984, 51–74.

Mitchell, R.C. and Davies, III, J.C. "The United States Environmental Movement and Its Political Context: An Overview." Mimeo, The Conservation Foundation discussion paper D-32, Washington, D.C., 1978.

Moore, G.T. "Knowing About Environmental Knowing: The Current State of Theory and Research on Environmental Cognition." (a review of the literature) *Environment and Behavior*, 1979b, *11* (1), 33–70.

Morrison, D.E. "The Environmental Movement Moves on—and Changes." Paper presented at the Purdue University Water Resources Seminar, 1972.

Morrison, D.E. "The Soft Cutting Edge of Environmentalism: Why and How the Appropriate Technology Notion is Changing the Movement." *Natural Resources Journal*, 1980, *20*, 275–298.

Morrison, D.E., Hornback, K.E. and Warner, W.K. "The Environmental Movement: Some Preliminary Observations and Predictions." In W.R. Burch, Jr., N.H. Cheek, Jr., and Taylor (Eds.) *Social Behavior, Natural Resources, and the Environment*. New York: Harper and Row, 1972, 259–279.

Murch, A.W. "Public Concern for Environmental Pollution." *Public Opinion Quarterly*, 1971, *35*, 100–106.

Murch, A.W. "Who Cares About the Environment?: The Nature and Origins of Environmental Concern." In A.W. Murch (Ed.) *Environmental Concern*. New York: MSS Information Corporation, 1974, 9–42.

Naess, A. "The Shallow and the Deep, Long Range Ecology Movement." *Inquiry*, 1973, *16*, 95.

Naroll, R. *The Moral Order: An Introduction to the Human Situation*. Beverly Hills: Sage Publications, 1983.

Nash, R. *Wilderness and the American Mind*. New Haven, Yale U. Press, 1967 (Rev. ed., 1973).

Nelkin, D. "Nuclear Power as a Feminist Issue." *The Environmentalist*, 1981 *23*, (Jan./Feb.).

Nelkin, D. and Pollak, M. "Political Parties and the Nuclear Energy Debate in France and Germany." *Comparative Politics*, 1980, *12* (2), 127–141.

Nelkin, D. and Pollak, M. *The Atom Besieged: Extra Parliamentary Dissent in France and Germany*. Cambridge, MA: MIT Press. 1981.

Odell, R. *Environmental Awakening: The New Revolution to Protect the Earth*. Cambridge, MA: Ballinger Publishing Company, 1980.

O'Riordan, T. "The Third American Conservation Movement: New Implications For Public Policy." *Journal of American Studies*, 1971, *5*, 155–171.

O'Riordan, T. "Public Interest Environmental Groups in the United States and Britain." *American Studies*, 1979, *13*, 409–438.

O'Riordan, T. *Environmentalism*. London: Pion, Ltd., 1981 (2nd edition). Published in the United States by Methuen, Inc., New York. (This work contains a 50-page bibliography covering works up to 1976 and an additional 6-page bibliography for works from 1976 to 1981.)

Passino, E.M. and Lounsbury, J.W. "Sex Differences in Opposition to and Support for Construction of a Proposed Nuclear Power Plant." In L.M. Ward, S. Coren, A. Gruft and J.B. Collins (Eds.) *The Behavioral Basis of Design*, Book 1. Stroudsburg, PA: Dowden, Hutchinson and Ross, 1976.

Passmore, J. *Man's Responsibility for Nature*. London: Duckworth. New York: Scribners, 1974.

Petulla, J.M. *American Environmentalism: Values, Tactics, Priorities*. Texas: A & M University Press, 1980.

Pierce, J.C. "Water Resource Preservation: Personal Values and Public Support." *Environment and Behavior*, 1979, *11* (2), 147–161.

Pirages, D. "A Framework for Analyzing Paradigm Maintenance and Change." Paper presented at the World Congress of the International Political Science Association, Rio de Janeiro, 1982.

Pirages, D. and Ehrlich, P. *Ark II: Social Response to Environmental Imperatives*. San Francisco: W. H. Freeman Press, 1974.

Rathbun, P.F., and Lindner, G. "Energy Needs vs. Environmental Values: Balancing of Competing Interests." Paper presented at the American Sociological Association Annual Meetings, New York, 1980.

Ray, J.R. "Environmentalism as a Trait." *The Planner*, 1974, *14*, 52–62.

Reed, J.H. and Wilkes, J.M. "Sex and Attitudes Toward Nuclear Power." Paper presented at the Annual Meeting of the American Sociological Association, 1980.

Ryan, B.F. *Social and Cultural Change*. New York: Ronald Press, 1969.

Saarinen, T.F. and Sell, J.L. "Environmental Perception." *Progress in Human Geography*, 1980, *4* (4), 525–548.

Sandbach, E. *Environment, Ideology and Policy*. Montclair, New Jersey: Allanfeld, Osmun, 1980.

Schnaiberg, A. *The Environment: From Surplus to Scarcity*. New York: Oxford University Press, 1980.

Schumacher, E.F. *Small is Beautiful: Economics as if People Mattered*. New York: Harper and Row, 1973.

Schwartz, P. and Ogilvy, J. *The Emergent Paradigm: Changing Patterns of Thought and Belief*. Menlo, CA: Stanford Research International, VALS Report #7, 1979.

Sewell, W.R.D. "Environmental Perceptions and Attitudes of Engineers and Public Health Officials." *Environment and Behavior*, 1971, *3*, 23–59.

Shaw, L.G., and Milbrath, L.W. "Citizen Participation in Governmental Decision Making: The Toxic Waste Threat at Love Canal, Niagara Falls, New York". Working paper series, Rockefeller Institute of Government, Albany, 1983.

Simon, R.J. "Public Attitudes Toward Population and Pollution. *Public Opinion Quarterly*, 1971, *35*, 93–99.

Skolimowski, H. *Eco-Philosophy: Designing New Tactics for Living.* Boston: Marion Boyars, 1981.

Slovic, P., Fischoff, B., and Lichtenstein, S. "Facts vs. Fears: Perceived Risk and Opposition to Nuclear Energy." Paper presented at the 148th Annual Meeting of AAAS, Washington, D.C., 1982.

Springer, J.F., and Costantini, E. "Public Opinion and the Environment: An Issue in Search of a Home." In S.S. Nafel (Ed.) *Environmental Politics.* New York: Praeger, 1974, 195–224.

Stallings, R.A. "Patterns of Belief in Social Movements: Clarifications from an Analysis of Environmental Groups." *Sociological Quarterly*, 1973, *14*, 465–480.

Tognacci, L.R., Weigel, R.H., Wideen, M.F., and Vernon, D.T.A. "Environmental Quality: How Universal is Public Concern? " *Environment and Behavior*, 1972, *4*, 73–86.

Tremblay, K.R., Jr., and Dunlap, R.E. "Rural-Urban Residence and Concern with Environmental Quality: A Replication and Extension." *Rural Sociology*, 1978, *43* (3), 474–491.

Tucker, W. "Environmentalism and the Leisure Class." *Harper's*, 1977, (December) 49.

Tucker, W. "The Environmental Era." *Public Opinion*, 1982a, *5* (1), 41–47.

Tucker, W. *Progress and Privilege: America in the Age of Environmentalism.* New York: Doubleday, 1982b.

Utrup, K. "Environmental Public Opinion: Trends and Tradeoffs, 1969–1978." Mimeo, Resources for the Future, Washington, D.C. 1978.

Utrup, K. "How Sierra Club Members See Environmental Issues." *Sierra*, 1979. (March-April), 14–18.

Valaskakis, K., and others. *The Conserver Society: A Workable Alternative for the Future.* New York: Harper and Row, 1979.

Van Liere, K.D., and Dunlap, R.E. "The Social Bases of Environmental Concern: A Review of Hypotheses, Explanations and Empirical Evidence." *Public Opinion Quarterly*, 1980, *44* (2), 181–197.

Van Liere, K.D., and Dunlap, R.E. "Environmental Concern: Does It Make a Difference How It's Measured? " *Environment and Behavior*, 1981, *13* (6), 651–676.

Watanuki, J. "Politics and Ecology in Japan." Paper presented to the Social Ecology section of the Tenth World Congress of Sociology, Mexico City, August, 1982.

Watkins, G.A. "Developing a 'Water Concern' Scale." *The Journal of Environmental Education*, 1974, *5* (4), 54–58.

Watkins, G.A. "Scaling of Attitudes Toward Population Problems." *The Journal of Environmental Education*, 1975, *7* (1), 14–26.

Watts, N., and Wandesforde-Smith, G. "Postmaterial Values and Environmental Policy Change." In D. Mann (Ed.) *Environmental Policy Formation: The Impact of Values, Ideology, and Standards.* Lexington, MA: D.C. Heath, 1981, 29–42.

Weigel, R.H. "Ideological and Demographic Correlates of Pro-Ecology Behavior." *Journal of Social Psychology*, 1977, *103*, 39–47.

Weigel, R.H., and Weigel, J. "Environmental Concern: The Development of a Measure." *Environment and Behavior*, 1978, *10* (1), 3–15.

Yankelovich, D. "New Rules in American Life: Searching for Self-Fulfillment in a World Turned Upside Down." *Psychology Today*, 1981 (April).

Yankelovich, D., and Lefkowitz, B. "National Growth: The Question of the 80's." *Public Opinion*, 1980a, *3* (December/January), 44–57.

Zetterberg, H.L. "Environmental Awareness and Political Change in Sweden." Paper prepared for a Conference on Environmental Awareness and Political Change, sponsored by the International Institute for Environment and Society (Berlin) and The Conservation Foundation (Washington, D.C.) in Berlin, January 1978.

INDEX